Hiding in
Unnatural
Happiness

Hiding in Unnatural Happiness

DEVAMRITA SWAMI

THE BHAKTIVEDANTA BOOK TRUST

The Bhaktivedanta Book Trust
PO Box 341445, Los Angeles, CA 90034 USA
Phone: +1-800-927-4152
Fax: +1-310-837-1056
E-mail: bbt.usa@krishna.com

The Bhaktivedanta Book Trust
PO Box 380, Riverstone, NSW, 2765, Australia
Phone: +61-2-9627-6306
E-mail: bbtaustralia@gmail.com
Web: www.bbt.org.au

United Kingdom: readerservices@pamho.net
Ireland: govindadvipa.info@gmail.com

"I Wish I Knew How It Would Feel to Be Free" (p. 25)
written by William Taylor, Richard Lamb
reprinted by permission of Duane Music Inc. (USA)

cover design by Amala Creative

ISBN 978-0-947259-86-0

Printed in China

Table of Contents

Preface · vii

Preface

Some people seem hard-wired for material success. Apparently on an endless winning streak, often since birth, they lead lives in a continual bubble bath of comfort, convenience, and gratification; they glory in wealth and acclaim.

Their polar opposites, at the dark end of the street, are the legions of the hard up and badly off. Seemingly born to lose, pinned under massive boulders of adversity, they experience only woe and punishing times.

The average Jane and Joe struggle to stay afloat in the storm-tossed middle class, dreaming of a secure upper perch while fearing falling back. They trudge dutifully through suburban routines, occasionally savoring peak feelings and gala moments.

"Anyway," we often hear, "money can't buy everything." Daily life, however, belies this old mantra. Happiness and even love often do seem to have a price tag, or at least a significant financial correlation. But whatever our level of income, we all long for happiness and well-being, however defined.

What about the special persons – those who, with wings of selfless magnanimity, soar beyond social pigeonholes?

Compassionate, empathetic, and noble, they radiate human sunshine in any kind of weather. Welcoming every encounter as an opportunity to benefit and nourish others, such heroes of the heart possess a magnetism of caring that makes them larger than everyday life. Their reason for living is to uplift; their life's mission, to inspire. They have found, somehow, inner fulfillment and peace.

Happiness, cheerfulness, satisfaction – however the subjective attainment is labeled – the twenty-first century has set off a gold rush to explain and attain it.

Happiness can be defined in a variety of different ways. Among them:

- An immediate, though short-term feeling of "life feels good"
- A zesty, though also short-lived psychological surge or jolt
- An upbeat, cheery disposition encoded in one's genes
- Sheer physicality and sensory stimulation
- The raw power of possession and control
- Capability and contentment
- Interpersonal connectivity and harmony
- Living in the moment and "letting life be"

Happiness scholar, UC Riverside professor, and author of *The How of Happiness*, Sonja Lyubomirsky, lets people define happiness their own way, but clinically, she analyzes it as "a combination of frequent positive emotions, plus the sense that your life is good."

Known as Dr. Happiness for his pivotal role in advancing the field, Edward Deiner, a founding father of research into subjective well-being, informs us that the pursuit of happiness confers sweeping benefits. "Happiness doesn't just feel good," he writes. "It's good for you and for society. Happy people are more successful, have better relationships, are healthier and live longer."

Moreover, Deiner wants us to know, "Materialism isn't bad. It's only bad if we use it to replace other things in life like meaningful work, a good marriage, kids and friends. People are recognizing that those who make money more important than love have lower levels of life satisfaction."

Martin Seligman, director of the Positive Psychology Center at the University of Pennsylvania and author of best-selling self-help books *Authentic Happiness*, *Flourish*, *and Learned Optimism*, describes the happiness search as a quest for activities that are absorbing and meaningful. Seligman defines "meaningful" activities as those that serve others, providing the doer with a sense of belonging to a cause greater than him or herself. You know you've found the Holy Grail, he says, when you become so engaged in whatever you're doing that you lose track of time. In a state of flow, you're "at one with the music."

Searching for hereditary clues to happiness in the laboratory, geneticists scrutinize our DNA. Meanwhile, neuroscientists peer into our brain, seeking the mystery of happiness by tracking neurochemical balances and imbalances.

Crunching research data, social scientists aim to construct nonsubjective measures for happiness. They dispel the popular belief that as nations increase their wealth, the citizens, benefiting from an improved quality of life, increase their happiness. The evidence shows that once societies attain a certain standard of living, happiness decouples from gains in wealth and luxury.

The present focus of Western happiness science generally lands on genetics. At least 50 percent of our personal sense of well-being, we are told, derives from our genetic makeup. Our circumstances, such as where you live or work, or your health or marriage – established situations that are difficult to change – weigh in at only 10 percent.

After the 60 percent predetermined by genetics and

curtailed by situations, our personal choices and will – the "Life is what you make of it" factor – come into play, for the remaining 40 percent.

This book explores another perspective, suggests a different road, one less traveled.

Beyond the material obstructions of genetics and circumstances, surpassing the tiny potential of our material intentionality and will, we can aspire for the realm of pure spiritual consciousness. On that route, we have 100 percent access to genuine happiness and well-being – for both the individual and society.

Hiding in Unnatural Happiness is a contemporary presentation founded upon ancient but timeless yoga knowledge – empowering us to shed the shackles of material assumptions and conditioning and enter a dimension of nonmaterial equal opportunity.

The first three brief articles kindle reaction and stir the pot of reflection. The next three get to the heart of humanity's happiness search by first identifying mass illusion and then the applied spiritual technology that can dispel it.

Expanded from lectures at universities, these longer articles challenge the narrow-minded material conceptions of the self and its satisfaction – fallacies that pervade the First, Second, and Third World.

Economics, politics, and environmentalism can only benefit from allying with a comprehensive wisdom culture. India's greatest export today is its nonmaterial information technology from deep in the past. Offering a scope and breadth of profound spiritual knowledge, this treasure of Eastern antiquity can revitalize the entire planet. India's *bhakti* texts in particular – presenting devotion in pure consciousness, the Love Supreme, as the ultimate goal of society – can transform our mismanaged human civilization.

Who can truly attain happiness? As stated in a graduate study of *bhakti-yoga*, *Srimad-Bhagavatam*, "Only two types of persons can be happy in this world. One is the completely enlightened, self-realized soul. The other is the tragically faithful servant of materialism, thoroughly focused upon exploiting temporary matter, in all its permutations, for fleeting gratification. Everyone else, in between these two classes, must experience some degree of anxiety."

Only a practiced and seasoned spiritual expert can be genuinely happy, thriving in the spiritual freedom of pure consciousness. Fully self-aware, at the pinnacle of the yoga and meditation system, such a connoisseur of enlightenment would never seek fulfillment in matter and its kaleidoscope of impermanence and hallucinogenic assurances.

On the other side are the stalwarts of illusion, passionately dedicated to "Ignorance is bliss; what you don't know won't hurt you." Dulled by the massive programming that so blankets society, mistaking bewilderment and delusion for happiness, such prisoners of deprivation – whether or not they are educated or wealthy – rarely think outside the box, beyond the body and mind.

Unthinkingly focused upon strenuous labor – whether industrial or corporate – meagerly rewarded by moments of mind-numbing entertainment and exploitative sensuality, such inwardly poor participants in our material culture cannot persevere without the artificial succor that intoxication delivers.

Those in between are neither proficient enough in spiritual knowledge and experience nor blind enough in ignorance and matter-mania. Consequently, due to uncertainty about their self and its place in existence, they experience inner anxiety and turbulence.

This book is aimed primarily at those halfway – the

neither fully enlightened nor the stubbornly bewildered. If advanced spiritualists happen upon this book, may their purity and grace uplift my efforts.

If the unfortunate but faithful servants of mass illusion turn the pages, may they glimpse a way out. I know what it is like, because I was once in that sheepfold. My heart goes out to its life members.

☙

Hiding in
Unnatural
Happiness

CHAPTER ONE

Stop the World,
I Want to Get On

Are you publicly pursuing routine material objectives but privately considering options off the beaten path? Are you unsure how your square pegs can fit into the round holes society seems to have predrilled for you? If so, it's time to go social-niche shopping. Search the aisles of society's supermarket for a role and a lifestyle that suit you. Is it your destiny to be a dedicated materialist, or an average apathetic Jane or Joe? Or maybe a spiritual dabbler, or even a committed traveler on a journey of self-discovery?

What would it even mean to explore the nonmaterial path? Would you shun the world of pleasure and pain as a dream, a mirage? Or would you embrace everything as divine and grab all the goodies you can? And what about your friends and family? Would they poke fun at you and treat your newfound zest with curious amusement – remind you that at some point you have to come back to the "real world"?

The truth is, you're just not sure. All you know is that you're tired of slogging through life with no knowledge of who you are or why you appeared in this world. An intuition of your true, inner identity coaxes you onward; you yearn for something more – a wholesome life and at least an introductory experience of some kind of higher awareness. But where can you find these? Where can you even look? Somehow you know that you won't be able to get the information you need from the mainstream scholastic knowledge factories and their assembly lines.

What is our place in this world – individually and as a species?

❧ *Humans: Expendable? Disposable?* ❧

Let's take a look at that "real world," the blend of economic, social, and sensual forces that mold us. The marketplace, consecrated as the standard for evaluating our lives, permeates our consciousness as we study, work, buy, consume, and die.

When we consider the place of humans in this world from a materialistic standpoint, we have no choice but to conclude that humanity is a total disturbance. The sad reality of our material relationship with the planet is summed up by one of the most important biologists of our time, Harvard emeritus professor Edward O. Wilson. "If all humanity disappeared," he writes, "the rest of life would benefit enormously. The biosphere would literally breathe a sigh of relief, as forests regenerated and endangered species revived."

At best, we are unnecessary, expendable. As Wilson says, the loss of any other species – ants, for instance – would result in "major extinctions of other species and probably partial collapse of some ecosystems." In terms of actual biomass, our presence is negligible – mathematically, the total mass of the human race could be stacked like sardines into

4

a space measuring just one cubic mile. Still, we reign supreme as habitat wreckers par excellence, the first species in the known history of life to become a geophysical force, having just in the last century altered the entire planet's chemical, biological, and physical balance.

We've stripped the forests, exhausted the soil, drained the water, and emptied the earth's natural resources. We've poisoned the land, the water, and the air with thousands of toxic chemicals, and dozens more lodge inside each of our bodies daily. Weather patterns range from unexpectedly peculiar to devastatingly extreme.

The price for this war of terror against nature will be punishing, far beyond anything we can predict. But instead of changing our climate, why not change our field of vision – lift it from the mass consumerism responsible for this global destruction, to a higher plane? It would be far better for nature's only disposable species to seek its purpose not in the materialism that threatens the planet's – and our – existence, but in spiritual development.

The ancient yoga texts of India champion the human form, with its developed consciousness, as a rare gift – specifically for the purpose of spiritual attainment. *Srimad-Bhagavatam* states:

> After innumerable births and deaths, we achieve the rare human form of life, which, though temporary, grants us the opportunity to attain the highest perfection. Therefore a sober human being should quickly endeavor for the ultimate perfection of life, as long as the body, always subject to death, has not expired. After all, sensory gratification is available even in the lowest and most gross species of life, whereas Krishna consciousness is possible only for a human being. (11.9.29)

The wealth of knowledge in this devotional yoga treasury – revered in India and now known throughout the world – explains what we have working for us:

Hiding in Unnatural Happiness

The human body, which can award all benefit in life, is automatically obtained by the laws of nature, although it is a very rare achievement. This human body can be compared to a perfectly constructed boat having a genuine guru as the captain and the instructions of the Supreme as favorable winds impelling it on its course. Considering all these advantages, a human being who does not capitalize on the human body to cross the ocean of material existence must be considered the killer of his own soul. (11.20.17)

❧ *Vanish or Transform?* ❧

From time immemorial, sages and saints have alerted us to the enormous human potential for spiritual progress latent in every individual and civilization. If we ignore that innate spiritual capability to transform ourselves, what is left for us? One answer comes from the Voluntary Human Extinction Movement, whose mission is to convince all humans to stop procreating, to "live long and die out," allowing the planet to return to a state "as close as possible to the Garden of Eden."

But while it may be true that our death as a species would mean life for others, our rugged determination to survive could actually help propel us through the dire straits of material disaster to an effective spiritual approach. Pressed by adversity, we could seek out an authentic cure for the greed, materialism, economic injustice, and environmental madness that so darken our present and future. Maybe we can improve the world around us and at the same time quell the thinly veiled turmoil within us.

Proponents of transformation can be categorized into two main schools of thought: "this-worlders" and "other-worlders." Other-worlders have their eyes on the prize, viewing our earthly habitation as just a training school for the celestial hereafter. Withdrawing from the temporal affairs of this temporary world, they concentrate on their own internal development.

Like mystic yogis in the Himalayas, the desert fathers of early Christianity, and some monks and nuns even today, other-worlders seclude themselves from the din of daily life, secure that all things will pass. Disenchanted by the despair and evil plaguing humanity, they may also pray and meditate for the well-being of all, as they prepare for what awaits us beyond – whether it be nirvana, heaven, the Vast Oneness, or the Great Unknown.

This-worlders live to embrace our existence on earth in toto, including all its joys and sorrows. Often avowed activists, humanitarians, and environmentalists, they plant their feet and keep their vision firmly on the ground – right here and now – in the belief that human vigor and aspiration focused on terra firma can improve life for billions of unfortunate people.

Aching to change the surrounding world economically, politically, and ecologically, this-worlders may resent the other-world perspective as a nuisance or, worse, an impediment. Why co-opt the amazing transformative potential of humanity – energy desperately needed for global renovation – and dreamily dissipate it into the clouds? As noted sociologist of secularism Phil Zuckerman writes, "[I]f you believe that this is the only world and there is no afterlife, that's going to motivate you to make it as good a place as

7

possible. ... [A]re we going to pray to end crime in our city or are we going to look at the root causes?"

∾ *Sacred Activism* ∾

To find comprehensive, satisfying answers to our questions, we must resolve the divide between "this" and "other" thinking and unite the inner and the outer, the here and the hereafter. It is a challenge met with consummate majesty by the yoga classic the *Bhagavad-gita*. The *Gita*, for short, is the standard authoritative text for the complete yoga ladder, presenting this-world yoga and other-world yoga interlinked.

Certainly, withdrawing from the world has its value. Who couldn't benefit from a personal retreat to recharge his or her batteries? Yet, our times demand global awareness of social, economic, and ecological crises.

Might there be a way that without our turning a blind eye to the world's demanding issues, we can acquire both freedom from the world and dynamic engagement with it? The *Gita* invites us to drink at the fount of *sacred* activism: the precise spiritual technology for truly being *in* the world but not *of* the world.

In Chapter 6 of the *Gita*, "The Yoga of Meditation," Krishna, the source of all yogic power, instructs, "The perfect yogi, by comparison to his own self, sees the true equality of all beings, in both their happiness and their distress" (6.32).

No doubt, some yogis opt for isolation and focus on their own elevation. But another type wants to benefit all living entities. These balanced, activist yogis, deriving spiritual strength from the inner world, scan the outer world – noting its grip of impermanent happiness and distress.

Striving for more than just their own perfect meditation, these sacred activists – masters of loving devotion, *bhakti-yoga* – reach out to change all dimensions of the planetary experience. Knowing with compassion the futile struggles of mundane existence, they aim for the complete welfare of all creatures. They observe the spiritual equality of all living entities, despite nature's parade of diverse biological and psychological costumes.

Still, a budding spiritualist may worry about living a vexing contradiction: "I now know I'm spiritual, but my whole life is focused on material affairs." *Srimad-Bhagavatam* addresses this conundrum, thoroughly analyzing the illusions that suffocate human society.

The *Bhagavatam* explains that the daytime of the materially overwhelmed person is devoted to complicated, often high-tech versions of basic Neanderthal pursuits. Hunting and gathering, we muscle and connive our way through the forest of education and employment.

When darkness falls, we seek release. We pin our hopes for redemption on a nocturnal brew of television, intoxication, and sex. The warm blanket of sleep grants us a temporary reprieve. But too soon, day breaks and the cycle of intense struggle resumes.

Why do we take what is so tedious, so deadening, so self-destructive and anoint it as the "real world"? How did we succumb to such low expectations of human potential, and how do we get out of the daily grind?

Gradually, the awareness will dawn on us that our highest spiritual aspirations and expressions are the essence of true human life, and the lifestyle of the genuine spiritual practitioner will triumph. A host of Krishna conscious adepts can testify how *bhakti-yoga* reorders a person's lifestyle and relationships so that the spiritual energies flowing from the Supreme can assume their rightful place.

This spiritual transformation culminates with entrance into divine vision and connectivity. In the *Bhagavad-gita*, Krishna Himself describes the actual real world:

A true yogi observes Me in all beings and also sees every being in Me. Indeed, the self-realized person sees Me, the same Supreme Personality, everywhere. For one who sees Me everywhere and sees everything in Me, I am never lost, nor is he ever lost to Me. (6.29–30)

Available in increments as a spiritual aspirant progresses, this attraction for the Supreme Source of Pleasure can reshape, transform our life. We begin to perceive that the world is a combination of material and spiritual energies emanating from Krishna, the ultimate fount. Those energies are neither ours to plunder or exploit nor ours to discard or negate.

Since everything, both matter and spirit, is the energy of the Supreme, we must hear from the Supreme how to engage it. A fundamental principle of sane existence is that we cannot concoct our own rules, our own style of interaction.

❧ *The Planetary Cancer* ❧

Today's deepening ecological crisis reveals that we are just too arrogant and tiny to handle material nature; we need a higher knowledge. Just think: half the world's tropical and temperate forests, and half of our wetlands, have vanished. Nearly half of our coral reefs have been destroyed or are on the brink of extinction. Oceans have lost an estimated 90 percent of their large predator fish, and 75 percent of fishing regions are either overfished or exploited to capacity. Every year, desertification overtakes land one and a half times the size of Greece.

Scientists estimate that by the end of this century, if the human impact on nature continues at the present rate, 20 to 50 percent of all living species will disappear. Our grandchildren may not see half the species of plants and animals that exist today.

Even conservative estimates predict that in the decades ahead, the pace of extinction, driven by climate change, will increase at least a thousand-fold. As journalist Elizabeth Kolbert documents in her Pulitzer-Prize-winning *The Sixth Extinction: An Unnatural History*, this fate is already upon us: species are currently disappearing at rates a thousand times faster than normal. Not in sixty-five million years – since the disappearance of dinosaurs – has Earth undergone biological extinction at such a grand scale. Earth's creatures are vanishing right before our eyes. Yet somehow, we accept this as normal, as the real world.

Agent Smith, the artificial intelligence construct in the film *The Matrix*, was created to stop enslaved humans from escaping the simulated reality the machines had built for them. Perhaps his searing tirade against humanity was not just fictional movie fare:

> I'd like to share a revelation that I've had during my time here. It came to me when I tried to classify your species and I realized that you're not actually mammals. Every mammal on this planet instinctively develops a natural equilibrium with the surrounding environment, but you humans do not. You move to an area and you multiply and multiply until every natural resource is consumed, and the only way you can survive is to spread to another area.
>
> There is another organism on this planet that follows the same pattern. Do you know what it is? A virus. Human beings are a disease, a cancer of this

planet. You're a plague and we [the machines] are the cure.

The global repercussions of our human handiwork are frightening. We have shown a destructive power that is expanding with no limit in sight, altering the natural features of an entire planet.

So, what to do? From the remote antiquity of spiritual India, sacred texts known as the Upanishads call: "Only a miserly person lives and dies like the cats and dogs – that is, never using the human potential to solve the puzzle of how to live, never grasping the science of self-realization."

Twenty-five hundred years ago, the classic Greek philosopher Socrates declared, "The unexamined life is not worth living." But the so-called "civilization" that dominates the world today is confident that it has proven the wise man wrong. Commandeering the best intelligence, contemporary human society enforces the grand solution: make money and indulge your senses on a global scale – lasting peace and prosperity will somehow follow.

Just half a century ago, Nobel laureate Albert Camus concluded, "There is only one truly serious philosophical issue: suicide – why not?" Be brave, he urged; put yourself on the spot. Is there any point to existence? Admit the absurdity, and then you can decide for yourself whether your life in the biosphere is worth sustaining.

My home base, New Zealand, has been rated by the United Nations as the most ecologically conscious nation in the world. And yet, surrounded by some of the most magnificent nature on Earth, one in six New Zealanders thinks annually of committing suicide, one in eighteen makes a plan, and one in twenty-two actually attempts it.

People hesitate to admit such behavior, so the numbers are likely much worse. In fact, suicide is the leading cause of death in New Zealand for ages twelve to twenty-five. "It's too peaceful here, too virgin and serene – our minds drive us crazy," small-town and rural youth complain. Even those who don't end their lives seek at least a temporary escape. "There's only one thing to live for," they say, "getting stoned, completely wasted, in the most awesome natural beauty."

❧ Welcome to the ·Real· Real World ❧

Should we deny life or affirm it? *Bhakti-yoga*, the timeless science of supramundane devotion, teaches us that, relying solely upon our own limited intelligence, we cannot decide. Likewise, justification to either reject or uphold the world lies beyond our tiny faculties. Since we, as bodies of matter housing particles of spirit, are energies of the Supreme, our human existence has an in-built prerequisite. For sane management of the energies composing us as well as surrounding us, we must take lessons from the Supreme Reality.

A surgeon's knife in the hand of a medical expert can accomplish great good, but that same tool in the hands of a murderer will unleash horror. A genuine spiritual practitioner seeks to neither reject the body nor indulge it, to neither coldly spurn the things of this world nor passionately embrace them. Rather than neglecting the world, the Krishna devotee engages with the world from the depths of an enlightened compassion, far beyond what the mundane mind can grasp.

The goal of authentic yoga and meditation is to take guidance from the source of all energies, the Ultimate Proprietor. Then humans can learn how to deftly use even the temporary material body and the temporary material world as springboards to spiritual freedom and global shift. Welcome to the real world. *Bhakti-yoga*, Krishna consciousness, is the perfection of the Information Age.

CHAPTER TWO

Walking the Forest of Unnatural Happiness

"I'm famished for satisfaction," the mind begs the body. "Make me feel like a natural enjoyer."

"Set us loose," the senses respond. They need no pleading. "We'll satisfy your every desire."

"I've worked hard for the right to enjoy," the mind computes. "I've earned it. Senses, lead me on – happy times are here!"

The Crucial Admission

Amazing opportunities open up for us when we admit that we don't know real happiness. Genuine human progress begins when we acknowledge our predicament, which is actually universal: our failure at material enjoyment. The struggle, the daily grind to squeeze true satisfaction from the rock of material nature, has cheated us. Wielding bodies and minds in countless lifetimes, we've gained only a mirage. But who would dare confess this?

When Hollywood megastar comedian Robin Williams took his life in 2014, the world took note. How could a man with everything – talent, wealth, fame, a cherished wife – wrap a belt around his neck and kill himself?" Once, walking off the stage to thunderous acclaim, his fans on their feet, Williams disclosed to talk-show host Dick Cavett, "Isn't it funny how I can bring great happiness to all these people, but not to myself?"

Less funny than tragic.

What may bewilder us even more is a report by social scientists measuring global happiness that a coolie carrying loads on his back through the streets of Kolkata experiences the same level of life-satisfaction as the average American.

How can we solve the riddle of real happiness? Brave minds abandon fantasies like "Be happy in your own way" and "Whatever gets you through the night." If the courageous, potential inner explorers, frustrated by today's predatory lifestyles, take the path of valor, they can do the most good for the outer world.

The reality check begins with classic honesty that cuts to the chase: "Never mind the media-hype; the hell with what people say – I don't think I actually know what is substantial or lasting happiness." This entry-level candor can swing the door open to real answers – to the timeless wisdom of the ancients. In the *Bhagavad-gita*, Krishna explains, "Now please hear from Me about the three kinds of material happiness by which the illusioned soul enjoys, and by which he sometimes comes to the end of all distress."

❧ *Material Happiness Laid Bare* ❧

Repeatedly stung and bitten in the forest of temporary enjoyment, how can we reach the end of suffering and despair? First, let's get an overview of Krishna's three categories of material happiness.

Type one is rare these days – virtuous goodness. Relished by those dedicated to mastering their own mind and senses, this topmost material happiness can lead further – to spiritual enlightenment. "In the beginning," Krishna tells us, it "may be just like poison, but at the end it is just like nectar ... and awakens one to self-realization" (*Bhagavad-gita* 18.37).

To the uneducated eye looking through the lens of material consciousness, a lifestyle of self-discipline and sense control can seem unattractively strict and rigorous – even repressive. Our vision victimized by hedonistic propaganda, we think the more we toss away the reins to our mind and senses – the more we let them stampede, consume, and cavort – the more pleasure we'll achieve.

But if we become determined practitioners of authentic yogic discipline, climbing steadfastly up the ladder of self-awareness, we can work through this misguided understanding and experience true inner calm and tranquility. This goodness of self-mastery, the highest level of material happiness, can then become a springboard for accessing the nonmaterial pleasure of the nonmaterial self in connection to the Supreme Self.

The second type of material happiness is the most common – passion: work hard, party hard – the grunt and groan approach to life, with the attractions of mind-numbing entertainment and sexual encounters, spiced by intoxication. It is a seductive process, hard for most people to resist. Happiness in passion, Krishna tells us, "derived from contact of the senses with their objects ... appears like nectar at first but poison at its end" (*Bhagavad-gita* 18.38).

Sooner or later, passionate, mundane accomplishments and sensual gratifications all lead to dissatisfaction, disappointment, and distress – even disaster, with the heavy price of depletion and dehumanization.

For most, the third, rock-bottom level of material

17

happiness is easier to reject, at least as a constant way of life. Krishna classifies it as ignorance – outright darkness from beginning to end, "blind to self-realization" (*Bhagavad-gita* 18.39).

Absorbed in this debased happiness – a type easily recognized as perverse – dedicated devotees of drink, drugs, and half-day sleeping waste their life. Lost in cloudlands of intoxication, inertia, and daydreaming, these most unfortunate persons are more self-destructive than even those driven to achieve and indulge on the hedonistic treadmill.

The everyday go-getter, committed to passion, pursues happiness in the routine slavish existence that consumer societies promote. Attracted by the mirage of material success, this false hero labors mightily to squeeze out some shadowy, insubstantial version of happiness. At the onset, these gutsy adventures seem sure to deliver their promised fulfillment, but the thrill inevitably fades, abruptly or gradually – morphing in the end into painful dismay. The temporary, false reprieve of intoxication – the weekend foray into ignorance – segues into the hung-over reality of Monday morning.

The hardcore inhabitant of happiness in lethargic ignorance fares much worse: aimlessness and intoxication almost 24/7. Not even a false ray of light beckons them onward. All is darkness and delusion – a wasteland from start to finish.

∾ *Genuine Heroics* ∾

Sometimes, however, a soul journeying through the matrix of these three flavors of material happiness, trapped in the maze of illusion, may reach the end, escape. And that greatest fortune can be yours – if you can count as your friends, your allies, experts who can expose the illusion for what it is and the naught it is worth.

The preeminent *bhakti* preceptor of our time, A.C. Bhaktivedanta Swami Prabhupada, world-renowned for his *Bhagavad-gita As It Is*, elaborates on what could happen to us while trekking through the forest of material fulfillment:

> A conditioned soul tries to enjoy material happiness again and again. Thus he chews the chewed. But sometimes, in the course of such enjoyment, he becomes relieved from material entanglement by association with a great soul. In other words, a conditioned soul is always engaged in some type of sense gratification, but when he understands by good association that it is only a repetition of the same thing, and he is awakened to his real Krishna consciousness, he is sometimes relieved from such repetitive so-called happiness. (*Bhagavad-gita* 18.36 commentary)

Yes, it can happen – real light at the end of the materialistic tunnel. But we don't get there by attempting to "thoroughly" experience material happiness. Endeavors to experience illusion simply grant us ... more illusion.

The night of the forest of self-deception finally turns to enlightening day when we associate with the right people – society's genuine heroes – living and thriving outside the stale materialistic mirage and inside a dynamic spiritual reality.

Come in from the storm. Directly from Krishna – the ultimate goal of all yoga and meditation – the wisdom-culture of nonmaterial life and happiness awaits you.

CHAPTER THREE

Hot for the Party That's Not: Dance to Keep from Crying

"You're too late."

Who savors that news? Flights missed, business opportunities squandered, romantic possibilities bungled – "too late" means time has hurtled onward, forcing us to accept outcomes ranging from routine inconveniences to devastating setbacks.

The roomful of South African university students peer at me silently, thoughtfully. Have I delivered the goods compassionately? They are processing.

These members of the "Rainbow Nation," mostly African, are burning with the desire to succeed. The barriers of apartheid now twenty years gone, their eyes are glued to what appears to be an open expressway ahead, and they're pressing the pedal to the floor.

Vroom, vroom!

Destination? The hype of material prosperity and happiness.

Craving a consumer paradise, my audience is desperate to join the First World in the soul-killing flames of material satisfaction. Like people throughout the developing world, these South African hopefuls feel they've stood by long enough. Now they want to take their place on the planetary stage of the materialistic bash. The global party-lights are flashing, bewitching – who can resist?

"Our ancestors died, the freedom fighters endured, and the national leaders connive," they say, "all to award us precious entrance to the party. Why just survive? Sense indulgence, gratification, is a basic human right. Let's get it on!"

But the midnight hour has long passed; the sun is about to rise: smashed furniture, broken bottles, stained carpets, drugged and drunken guests colliding or collapsed in stupor, an argument here, vomiting there, sad hookups everywhere.

"You've arrived too late," I inform my audience. The all-night rave, one hell of a hedonistic blast, is over.

Politicians everywhere promise to rake the dying embers, reigniting the wildfires of materialistic hopes. But the gap between the haves and have-nots – the 1 percent and the 99 percent – continues to widen. It's a worldwide no-win situation for everyone.

Meanwhile, maddened by the fever of false progress, we've trashed the planet. Our environmental woes are publicized daily, but we can't find the collective motivation to change course.

"Admit it," I beg them, "the revelry is finished. A long shot is the only hope – fire up an after-party! Rally a group of come-latelies and rekindle the flames – frantic, flickering, futile.

Let's dance amidst our tears.

My challenge to the students: Why seek to beat the dead horse? Why compete for the chance to chomp what the First World has already thoroughly chewed? Don't swallow it, I plead. Let's start anew – build this new nation on a spiritual platform.

As the erudite *bhakti-yogi* Prahlada Maharaja states in

Srimad-Bhagavatam, "Because of their uncontrolled senses, persons too addicted to materialistic life make progress" (7.5.30). But to where? Their achievement is evermore complicated, unsolvable distresses, both individually and socially. They "make progress toward hellish conditions and repeatedly chew that which has already been chewed," energetically, munching on the remnants of previous generations. Consequently, their dormant inclinations toward nonmaterial lifestyles, leading to the all-attractive spiritual reality, "are never aroused."

We can no longer buy into the usual promises of material analyses. We need a new, solution-focused generation to grace the earth – a new wave that strives to make a real difference by analyzing human problems and comprehending that they are never truly solved on the same materialistic level that gave rise to them.

Real human progress kicks in when the mirage, the mass consensual trance, loses its attraction. When the constant stream of our material attempts exhaust us, when we are weary of the illusory matrix of consumer culture – that is when our actual advancement in real human life finally begins.

In the *Bhagavad-gita*, Krishna assures us that even if we are the most deluded of hardcore materialists, acting as if nothing exists other than matter and its movements and modifications, "when you are situated in the boat of transcendental knowledge, you will be able to cross over the ocean of miseries," the ocean of perpetual material bafflement and unrest (4.36).

Transcendental knowledge means information and education beyond that which has a beginning and an end, which is beyond the permutations and adaptations of physiology and psychology. What the *Gita* grants us exceeds the limited, temporal domain of time and space.

Krishna goes on to declare that we'll never find in this world any prosperity or acquisition as sublime and pure as nonmundane, transcendental wisdom. Simply by seeking to understand who Krishna is – through authenticated, non-material processes – we will walk away with what no financial market indices can measure. Our priceless treasure is irrevocably beyond the gains and losses, booms and busts, of temporary material existence.

" There is nothing so sublime and pure," Krishna tells us, "as transcendental knowledge. Such knowledge is the mature fruit of all mysticism." And the genuine yogi, accomplished in *bhakti* – the yoga of ultimate connection – experiences and enjoys this knowledge within (*Bhagavad-gita* 4.38).

Rather than saluting a wannabe civilization insistent on partying itself to death, we can join the wise, who've had enough. We can work to eradicate the material illusion – both individually and en masse. And when we do, the time-less spiritual art, science, and culture that emanate from Krishna, the infinite Superconsciousness, awaits us, the minute particles of consciousness.

"One should meditate upon the Supreme Person as the one who knows everything, as He who is the oldest, who is the controller, who is smaller than the smallest, who is the maintainer of everything, who is beyond all material conception, who is inconceivable, and who is always a person. He is luminous like the sun, and He is transcendental, beyond this material nature" (*Bhagavad-gita* 8.9).

After focusing in this way, we can advance to the last stop in our quest for the most profound and comprehensive spiritual knowledge: awareness of Krishna as the Supreme Beloved and Enjoyer.

❧

CHAPTER FOUR

Freedom: Fantasy and Fact

Expanded from a presentation at the University of the Witwatersrand in Johannesburg, South Africa, March 20, 2014.

∾

> *I wish I knew how it would feel to be free.*
> *I wish I could break all the chains holding me.*
> *I wish I could say all the things I could say.*
> *Say them loud, say them clear,*
> *For the whole round world to hear.*
> *I wish I could share*
> *All the love that's in my heart*
> *Remove all the bars that keep us apart.*

Freedom is an aspiration that resonates with all human beings. We can approach it from many angles: political, economic, intellectual, religious, academic, artistic ... As individuals, we prize freedom of movement; as a group, freedom of assembly. Whenever we hear that something is free, we get a sense of no boundaries, no curbs: free elections, free markets, free love, free thinking.

Marketing experts milk our love of freedom and free things. Go to a store and what do you see? "Buy two, get the third one free." Consumer marketers know that although you really don't need more than one, you can't resist the temptation of getting something for free. You rationalize, "I came to purchase only one, but look at this deal – maybe I could stockpile the other two, or give them to family."

We are drawn to freedom and anything free. Yet we should attempt a deeper understanding of freedom – how we conceptualize it and how we live it.

Nelson Mandela once said, "There's no such thing as part freedom." But what have our economic and political leaders been offering the world? Part freedom at best.

We need to increase our understanding of freedom, strengthening it based not on material dreams but on spiritual reality. Working to accomplish that goal, my teacher and guide, Srila A. C. Bhaktivedanta Swami Prabhupada, visited South Africa in 1975. He also traveled to Kenya and spoke at the University of Nairobi, where he exhorted the students, faculty, and government officials to build their nation on the spiritual platform:

"I invite all intelligent Africans to come and understand this philosophy and distribute it. You are trying to develop yourselves, so please develop spiritually, for spiritual development is sound development. Don't imitate the Americans and Europeans ... Such civilizations built on the consciousness of sense gratification cannot stand."

If we are ever to attain real progress, we must consider the spiritual dimension. Only then can we make sense of what is full – not partial – freedom.

In the aftermath of World War II, humanity struggled to recover from its mass trauma. Fifty-five million people had perished. The years following brought to light horrific accounts of atrocities and genocide, alongside mighty plans for redesigning and rebuilding. The resounding postwar global resolve: "Never again!"

Nations of the world came together and approved the United Nations Charter and the Universal Declaration of Human Rights. Assembled emissaries formulated a list of inviolable, non-negotiable rights, so that even a majority in a democratic country could not vote to breach them. In this way, the world's leaders thought to clear a monumental path for the future progress of all humanity.

Without rights, how can freedom exist? And without freedom, how can humanity achieve lasting progress?

◈ The Mythic Quintet: Contemporary Concoctions of Human Progress ◈

Impeding our grasp of freedom are a set of quintuplets. Born of the same faulty intelligence, these five embody awesome, if suspect, myths of human progress.

Myth #1: Money brings happiness. Social scientists have established that increases in income or luxury beyond a basic middle-class standard of living do not lead to an increase in happiness. When I asked an audience of two hundred students and professors at the University of Cape Town if they knew of this finding, about 80 percent raised their hand. But when I inquired, "Knowing this, and knowing your own level of intelligence and potential, how many of you expect to voluntarily live your life at only a basic middle-class standard?" Not a single hand went up.

The disparity between the two responses demonstrates a problematic split – a worrisome disconnect – between supposed knowledge and actual lifestyle, between the knowledge we think we have and the knowledge we actually possess. Real knowledge is evidenced in our actions. If our actions do not reflect what we think we know, then we don't actually know it – we are, and we live, in ignorance.

Myth #2: Technology brings well-being. Contributing to our status as economic-growth fanatics, we've become acolytes in the Church of Technology, enthusiastically embracing applied science as the shelter, indeed savior, of human civilization. Meanwhile, the all-important internals of genuine human welfare are fading. Since the onset of the Industrial Revolution and through the Information Age, technology has held an esteemed place in human society. But can we truthfully say that our technologically complicated lives are qualitatively better – especially in terms of freedom from anxiety, freedom from stress? And what about internal wholesomeness – a happy heart and a peaceful mind? Mental depression is now the second most impactful disease worldwide, with its greatest occurrence in the materially advanced First World.

Myth #3: Weapons bring security – has a major impact on the global past, present, and future. The United States, for example, in the fiscal year 2014, spent 18 percent of total government revenue on defense and security related international ventures. Somehow, voters and taxpayers there are convinced that all this military spending – 650 billion dollars – is a noble and necessary price to pay for safety and protection in an unpredictable world. The United States, spending 40 percent of the world's military expenditures, is the world's biggest exporter of major arms, accounting for 31 percent of the global tally.

Myth #4: The earth provides virtually unlimited resources for our exploitation. We live as if we have several planet Earths – global overshoot: using more of the planet's resources than it can replenish. Why worry about the ecological state of the world we're leaving to our children? We've paid our dues, struggled to get or stay ahead – our kids can pay theirs. Human ingenuity will always triumph; future generations will come up with something, the latest and the greatest, to fix all the environmental havoc we've wrought. After all, isn't that what progress is all about?

And myth #5: We have a limitless planetary capacity for absorbing byproducts, waste, trash. The predominant notion is that after we've plundered the gifts of nature, following myth #4, the earth then graciously offers humanity a boundless sink, dump site, for our industrial and consumer waste.

Consider the ecological journey of just one item: plastic. The Yale University school of environmental studies, the oldest in the United States, reports that the past decade alone produced as much plastic as did the entire twentieth century. Now spread throughout the world's oceans, a plastic "soup" has developed its own unique ecosystem, which scientists have dubbed the "plastisphere." Estimates for the time nature needs to break down plastic debris range from five hundred years to one thousand years to "Who knows?" Even plastics that break down quickly offer no solace. While disintegrating, they leach toxic chemicals into the ocean.

☙ Freedom from Fables ☙

Let's face the music: this myth-quintet has betrayed us and bound us in chains. But what is real freedom, to replace the counterfeit? The timeless knowledge Krishna transmits in the *Bhagavad-gita* identifies our authentic needs. Lacking a correct awareness of the self and its primary necessities, we'll never escape the timeworn traps of materialistic economics, politics, and lifestyles. In any human society, of course, economic and political components are

29

necessary. But when these mundane structures become ends unto themselves in a world of their own, human society is in trouble – despite – or because of – technological proliferation.

We've come to a time when the greatest concepts of material life are both suspect and shaky. Even the hallowed Western ideal of democracy based on economic growth, the bedrock of many of our concepts of freedom, is wobbling. The most recent issue of *The Economist* magazine, which often sets the party line for international news media, highlights a special feature: "Democracy Is in Trouble."

Political scientists have noted that the last quarter of the twentieth century boasted a great peak for democratic exultation. The breakup of the Soviet Empire, the end of apartheid in South Africa, and other events heralded what many have deemed a democratic juggernaut.

Alas, life is what happens while experts are busy making plans and projections, and at least for now, the tide has changed – political studies reveal that the global impact of democracy is receding.

What has sent the tide the other way? There are two main causes. First, the global financial crisis that started in 2008. Democracy could not prevent that. Moreover, democracy could not effectively reform the banking system – or the bankers themselves. The effect on the world was not only financial but also psychological: confidence plummeted.

But there's a greater contributor to the democratic decline. China is showing that freedom of expression, speech, and thought is not requisite or even important – economic acceleration is the be-all and end-all of solutions. Lawrence Summers, former chief economist at the World Bank and former US secretary of the treasury, explains the bottom line: when America was at its economic peak, doubling its standard of living took thirty years; China does that every ten years. The creed is growth – economic expansion achieved by any means, except Western political ideals.

Chinese leaders are, of course, quite upbeat: "What's all the prattle about freedom?" they challenge. "Western values and political systems produce disorder and mayhem, especially in the developing world. Where is the Western world's economic power now? Professional managers, experts – not voters – decide what is most beneficial. We make our citizens an offer that none refuse: The Party stays in power and the Chinese people prosper."

Freedom: Fantasy and Fact

Up-and-coming nations around the world, such as Dubai, Vietnam, and Rwanda, aspire to imitate the Chinese model. And indeed, if the goal of society is economic advancement, why not? Political programs are less important than consumer economics; affluence is more seductive than traditional notions of freedom and rights.

Go to China and you see gleaming airports, brand new highways, superfast transport systems. People around the world are thinking, "This is what we want – the white waters of the economic rapids. We can live without Western fantasies of freedom if we can have the prosperity of a consumer society."

Chinese leaders are confident they've found the silver bullet. Their leaders and mainstream intellectuals openly say, "What is the use of your democratic systems? You elect incompetents and sweet-talkers while we assemble and groom the brightest, most competent leaders. Look what we provide the people through our policies of control."

By its own admission, China is an environmental disaster. The costs of its economic miracle are horribly polluted air, soil, and water. People wear surgical masks just to walk the streets. Meanwhile, the governmental elite could use some lessons from Confucius regarding virtue, simple

31

living, and self-sacrifice. The Chinese upper crust have become a self-perpetuating and self-serving in-crowd. *The Economist* reveals that the fifty richest members of the China's National People's Congress are collectively worth $94.7 billion – sixty times as much as the fifty richest members of America's Congress.

❧ *Missing in Action: Precise Spiritual Knowledge* ❧

This model of economic advancement at all costs reflects a misguided, mistaken understanding of what is best for the human being. A few thousand years ago, Plato pointed out democracy's Achilles heel: populist proposals that focus on short-term gain can whip up the people and sweep them away. And the pundits at *The Economist* agree: Plato had that right. But the knower of Vedic knowledge – conversant with what transcends the material domain – penetrates to a deeper bedrock.

In the *Bhagavad-gita*, Krishna explains that as long as we think ourselves as matter, as long as we lack awareness of our spiritual identity, we are controlled by illusion. Failing to grasp that the top priority is enlightenment, society must suffer – all efforts for sustainable progress will be thwarted.

Of course, we must care for our material needs, and certainly we should strive to alleviate the damage from perennial economic and political injustice. But while coping with these external priorities, we have forgotten the power of our spirit souls. And beyond even that, we have forgotten our connection to the Ultimate Soul. Neglecting to investigate our nonmaterial identity, we struggle, seeking fulfillment through the various conglomerations of matter. Some may talk sentimentally about our spirituality, our spiritual self, but where is the definitive scientific knowledge of the spirit soul, and what is the spiritual technology of how to experience it?

Unless we have a class of leaders who can uplift the people with applied spiritual knowledge, we will always see societies rise, show some bluster, and then stumble and fall. Restructuring and revolution, autocracy and democracy, come and go.

When we view the progress of the planet as a whole, the march of the centuries reveals that even as various nations ascend and decline, the global human condition does not change. No amelioration is enduring or significant enough to warrant materialistic faith or optimism.

Thanks to the media industry and expert politicians, change can seem just a campaign promise or a sudden coup away. But while in terms of the externalities of society, adjustment does happen, it's just a reshuffling of the same deck, first this way, then that, and we all know what happens after the initial bold hopes and intoxicating exuberance fizzle out. Feeling let down, left behind, and left out, the people plunge from elation into frustration, cynicism, and then dangerous rage.

For the most part, political change simply means that the ins become the outs and the outs become the ins – while hidden financial titans and conglomerates hold the strings. Amidst this continual game of musical chairs and puppeteering, what can thoughtful human beings do to focus on their real needs?

❧ *Five Levels of Experiencing the Supreme* ❧

Vedic philosophy gives us a way by which we can visualize the Supreme Absolute Truth in our everyday lives. There are five levels – three in the domain of material nature,

33

ordinary material existence, and two that are transcendental – beyond matter, space, and time. Without a grasp of the top two of the five levels, we cannot truly benefit humanity – or ourselves.

The terms for these levels come from Sanskrit, a language particularly appropriate for discussing enlightenment. Every language has its strength – English for business, German for science, and French for romance. Sanskrit is the language of spiritual science.

The first level of experiencing the presence of the Supreme in one's life is called *anna-maya:* realization of God based on food.

Upon the passing of Nelson Mandela, the UN's Food and Agriculture Organization praised him for his understanding that so much of freedom depends on food, and not simply on growing it but also on its distribution. The UN has calculated that one third of all the food produced in the world is wasted: 1.3 billion metric tons annually. Of all the fruits and vegetables grown in the United Kingdom, 30 percent is wasted merely because it doesn't look good enough for consumers. And when food does make it to our table, we can't control our eating. So even as one billion people in the world are starving, another billion are obese. Obviously, there's a crisis in both distribution and self-control.

The basic awareness that our lives are maintained by food is a preliminary appreciation of God – we cannot maintain ourselves. People often say grace at the table before eating, thanking the Lord for His bounty. "Food on my table; I know my God is able." Such God-realization is quite rudimentary, but it is noteworthy nonetheless – a beginning.

The second level of God-realization is *prana-maya:* understanding God through our breath – the fact that we're breathing, that we're alive. Again, rudimentary yet commendable. It refers to cognizance of the Supreme by virtue of our life-force.

In my travels spanning the continents, I have seen many places where people are terrorized by injustice and barbarism. "Will I be imprisoned?" they wonder. "Will I be brutalized?" Even, "Will we be victims of genocide?" So just as we don't want to minimize the first level, *anna-maya* – gratitude for sustenance – we also don't want to undervalue *prana-maya* – thankfulness to God for our every breath, enabling us to live another day. Both levels are legitimate, even important, preliminaries to spiritual science.

The perceptive person is keenly aware of the fragility of material existence – our dependency, our helplessness. Life in a material body, with a material mind, means that whether you're rich or poor, your existence is vulnerable. A reflective, humble person can detect the presence of God in these first two basic facets of existence.

The third, and last, preliminary level is *jnana-maya* – appreciating God because we can think, we can intuit, we have cognition. Universities today have become factories for the factories, training grounds for unabashed careerism and financial gain. But the classical view of higher education – the university, that hive of material intelligence – is that it bestows culture upon you, distilling your thinking and refining your sensibilities.

Human beings need intellectualism, and we can appreciate the presence of the Supreme Absolute Truth just through our thought processes. To quote Descartes's famous axiom, "I think therefore I am." Those devotedly pursuing material knowledge, however, should question its overall purpose.

Srila Prabhupada, a teacher of spiritual intelligence, compassionately alerted the world to the futility of pursuing only material knowledge. He rearticulated, for our current times, the ancient Vedic conclusion warning humans not to waste their higher faculties by focusing on manipulating material nature. If we forget the most important science, knowledge of the unit of spiritual consciousness, known in Sanskrit as the *atma,* we squander our precious human form of life.

✎ *Beyond the Material* ✎

Fortunately, there are two levels of spiritual realization that surpass the preliminary three. The spiritual treasures associated with ancient India urge us to reach past the lower phases of temporary mind and body and begin on level four: *vijnana-maya.*

In the *Bhagavad-gita,* the Song of the Supreme Opulent One, Krishna, presented as the Supreme Source, the Absolute Truth, the Ultimate Reality, reaches out to us through a dialogue with the spiritually noble Arjuna. Assuming a state of bewilderment to facilitate our instruction, Arjuna presents to Krishna the most astute, succinct material analyses of potential outcomes. Yet Krishna completely deflates them. He instructs that, though Arjuna is speaking words of erudition, he is absorbed in unworthy considerations, hung up on temporary bodies of matter (*Bhagavad-gita* 2.11).

Krishna acknowledges the brilliance of Arjuna's materially based sociological and political insights, but in brushing those perspectives aside, He discounts even the conventional religious angles that Arjuna proffers. They are matter-bound, He says, fleeting and flickering like the body itself. Krishna wants to emphasize that the best material knowledge, and even materially affected religion, cannot compare to pure knowledge of the soul. Mundane intelligence, knowledge of temporary material affairs and interactions, can never supplant authoritative spiritual science.

We have an eternal spiritual identity different from the body and mind. On the *vijnana-maya* level, we enter the realm of authentic spirituality, where we can start to experience the existence and power of our nonmaterial self, the soul. This is where real freedom begins.

The pinnacle of human achievement is level five: *ananda-maya*. It is the crown of consciousness and its development: relishing the love supreme, the dynamic relationship between us, the individual souls, and the Supreme All-attractive, of which we're part.

In the *Bhagavad-gita*, Krishna personally invites us to this relationship, which will finally satisfy our core being. "Because you are My very dear friend," He tells Arjuna – and us – "I am speaking to you My supreme instruction – the most confidential knowledge of all. Hear this from Me; it is for your benefit.

Always think of Me, become My devotee, worship Me and offer your reverence to Me. Consequently you will certainly come to Me. I promise you this because you are My very dear friend (18.64, 65)."

Now we have arrived at the ultimate goal of yogic knowledge, the most important instruction in all the vast Vedic spiritual texts. No amount of altering material nature – no material construction, deconstruction, or reconstruction – can ultimately satisfy the individual or society, because our real problem is disconnection from the Supreme.

The precise meaning of the word *Krishna* is "the unlimited all-attractive source of pleasure." In the *Bhagavad-gita*, He claims all living beings, no matter what species, as His children. Yet, overwhelmed by material existence, we have forgotten our real purpose in life: how to become truly free through divine dependency – the real goal of yoga knowledge.

Hiding in Unnatural Happiness

In the twenty-seven years that Nelson Mandela spent in prison during the apartheid regime, he learned – and taught others – how to survive in the penal system. According to a prisoner's perceived ethnicity – white, Indian, mixed, or African – he or she would receive a certain standard of food. Whites got the best; Africans, the worst; and the others, in between. Moreover, based on periodic evaluations of tractability, prisoners were designated as a class A, class B, class C, or class D.

Many of the younger anti-apartheid activists were defiant, refusing to acknowledge their captors and disregarding their commands, but Mandela, older and more strategic, worked to convince them: "Be tactful and shrewd; this prison will probably be your home for quite some time."

Accepting that in their circumstances, discretion was indeed the better part of valor, the young militants gradually heeded Mandela, and he negotiated with the prison staff, systematically extracting adjustments that made the prisoners' backbreaking lives in prison just a bit more bearable.

Even though the men seemed to be making compromises to improve their conditions, they always kept their vision on their struggle for freedom. They established clandestine communication links with activists on the outside and formulated plans for how to govern a new South Africa, liberated from the scourge of apartheid.

Their example throws light on how we can engage ourselves in the material world even while planning for our future beyond it. We are spirit souls, pure conscious entities, entrapped in temporary material bodies in a temporary material world. In his commentary to *Srimad-Bhagavatam*, Srila Prabhupada eloquently explains our condition:

The need of the spirit soul is that he wants to get out of the limited sphere of material bondage and fulfill his desire for complete freedom. He wants to get out of the covered walls of the greater universe. He wants to see the free light and the spirit. That complete freedom is achieved when he meets the complete spirit, the Personality of Godhead. There is a dormant affection for God within everyone; spiritual existence is manifested through the gross body and mind in the form of perverted affection for gross and subtle matter. Therefore we have to engage ourselves in occupational engagements that will evoke our divine consciousness. (1.2.8 commentary)

While arranging to live suitably, comfortably, we should not in any circumstances forget our preeminent priority. Humanity's prime concern must be liberation from material illusion and reconnection with our all-perfect Origin. Yes, we must strive to live with justice and dignity, but let's keep our eyes fixed on the prize. Real freedom is not on the material plane. That we are units of spiritual consciousness means that real freedom is in the spiritual realm. Until we can access that, we'll always be baffled and frustrated.

Nelson Mandela also stated, "Man's goodness is a flame that can be hidden but never extinguished." But how good are we? And how good can we be? We need transcendental knowledge – intelligence beyond the material – to inform us. Then we can understand the true and full potential of the human being. The flame seems hidden because we can't perceive our spiritual identity by material methods – so we ignore it. Blind to our true nature, we become easy prey for manipulation, both by the external demands of the socio-political schemes of our so-called "leaders," and by the internal, though artificially induced, desires of our own contaminated minds.

Comprehensive nonmaterial knowledge is essential – of both the full, true nature of the self, and the identity of the Ultimate Reality of which we are part. Promise the people this kind of knowledge, equip them with applied spiritual technology, and they won't succumb to shady assurances of economic acceleration, which even if could last, cannot possibly yield real or lasting satisfaction.

No amount of material gain will lead us to this goal. In any case, the planet will not fulfill humanity's ever-increasing material desires. The earth will never provide the resources to match our raging appetite; nor has it the capacity to assimilate our wastes. Thinking outside the materialistic box is not just a good exercise – it is an absolute, critical necessity.

Clearly, we must adopt a different approach, take another route. Yes, we should correct corruption as well as faulty politico-economic systems and their leaders. But while we duly strive to cope with material existence, let us not become obsessed with changing from one class of prisoner to another, forgetting that we have a precious chance for real life outside the prison. Human life is the conduit to full freedom: the liberty of the spirit self in relationship to the Supreme Self.

This is the knowledge Krishna gives, the same essential information Srila Prabhupada came here to deliver: to rebuild Africa – and the world – on the spiritual platform. Amidst all economic and political endeavors and ongoing problems, we must not forget our real self – the spirit soul – and our eternal relationship to the Supreme All-Attractive Source.

Our materialistic mantra – "Work, buy, consume, die" – has manacled us, imprisoned the whole world. What a tragedy. If we turn to leaders who cannot offer any higher goal than the hedonistic treadmill, we can be sure that there will be no solution to human problems – neither today nor tomorrow.

It's not too late. But we must consider another methodology. Yes, we must take care of our body and mind. But such endeavors, though necessary, are secondary. Remember, humanity's birthright is to pursue full, not just partial, freedom. And that will happen only if we apply the full science of spiritual development.

Freedom: Fantasy and Fact

CHAPTER FIVE

Spiritual Economics

*Expanded from a talk given at the Rotman School of
Management, University of Toronto, May 29, 2007.*

⟡

Born in New York City, a citizen of both the United States
and New Zealand, I like to consider myself a tenant of the
world. One of the global regions where I spend time is the
former Soviet bloc. Especially in present Russia, where a
few people have prospered fantastically, I've encountered
some of the older population who long for what they now
recall as benign aspects of the old Soviet days. I haven't met
anyone who would deny the political and religious oppres-
sion of those ferocious years, but there are also memories of
a kind of stability, predictability, and security missing today.

Cross an ocean to the United States, and we find that
especially since the financial crisis of 2008, people are
scratching their political-economic heads and wondering,
"Could there be an alternative beyond classic smokestack
socialism and boom-bust capitalism? Can we devise a better,
more wholesome way?" Meanwhile, in social-welfare states
such as New Zealand, Australia, and the United Kingdom,
people worry, "Will the government money be there for us?"

43

Unless people can tap into a higher dimension of existence, they will remain trapped by the usual lower-level motivations that have proved so problematic. I want to advocate an economic culture based not on getting but on giving. Such an overhaul of human motives would necessitate a distinctly transcendent methodology and worldview.

Ancient yoga texts explain that self-interest is at work in both the material and spiritual domains. And we can see today that it plays an extraordinary role not only in free markets, but also in genuine spiritual development. As Krishna explains in the *Bhagavad-gita*, only with the superior experience of the Supreme Reality will we slacken our grip on our inferior, materialistic lifestyle.

But how can we change our societal and individual habits so that our economic affairs encourage rather than deaden the highest aspirations of the individual and society?

There has recently been an outburst of research on prosperity, happiness, and choice, with one central question: In today's context of free-market democracies, are people actually becoming happy? Could it be that as a society grows wealthier and people have more material choices, their happiness levels remain the same or even decline? Indeed, the research points in this direction – and the resulting implications are significant.

When human beings engage in economic affairs, they seek to satisfy their perceived needs and wants. But what happens when in a developed economic culture, the satisfaction sputters and stalls?

In the United States, the gross domestic product (GDP) has more than doubled in the last forty years, but the proportion of the population describing themselves as very happy has declined by 5 percent. In Japan, the GDP has quintupled, yet the number of people who describe themselves as very happy has remained the same or dipped.

These realities spur scholars to question the fundamentals – the foundations underlying human economic activity. We assume that people, beyond meeting their needs, strive to satisfy their wants. But now we're discovering that in the most affluent, want-conscious nations, happiness has flatlined or even declined. Specifically, as the opulence of choice increases, people become less content.

The late Nobel laureate Herbert Simon of Carnegie Mellon – a psychologist and economist, the latest combination – coined the term *satisficers*. Satisficers are consumers who live life satisfied that their consumptive choices have been "good enough." They think, "I've sufficiently considered all the options and angles and have made what I consider to be a reasonably good choice. Let's leave it at that and move on."

Barry Schwartz, professor of social theory and social action at Swarthmore College, contrasts these satisficers with what he calls *maximizers*: people who constantly scrutinize, evaluate, and reconfigure their options, ceaselessly striving to make the best possible choice at every moment, every step in life. This is the average Joe and Jane that our materialistic society praises and promotes.

When satisficers find an item or option that suits their expectations, they stop searching. It's not that they are lazy and apathetic; they have just made their choice and moved on. Maximizers, however, continue to choose and choose again, without cease.

How do you know if you are a maximizer? Schwartz lists a set of qualifications:

1. When faced with a choice, you map out all the possibilities, including those not currently present or relevant.
2. Even if you are reasonably satisfied with a choice or situation, you stay on your toes, alert for something better.

45

3. When listening to the radio or watching TV, you station hop and channel surf, searching for a superior offering.
4. In relationships, you shop around, thinking that the more potential partners you sample, the greater the chance of your hitting upon Mr. or Ms. Right.

5. Buying gifts for a relative or friend is an ordeal. You've got to get it just right.
6. Choosing movies, cafés, and holidays – or shopping for clothes, furniture, and health supplements – is a stressful drama. The perfect choice is out there, somewhere, and you have to find it.
7. You cherish lists that rank things. Who are the hundred greatest sports stars, the fifty most influential people, last year's twenty-five biggest flops? When you are shopping, especially through online mega-outlets, how many stars have buyers given an item?
8. You never accept second best or second place. Even if something you do or get seems sufficient – your desire for perfection is insatiable. After all, you believe, you have only one body, one life, one opportunity.

In short, a maximizer's life is defined by constant product comparison, both before and after acquisition. As the choices in society increase and the information about each choice expands, decision-making becomes more and more daunting. When practicality forces maximizers to end their search, or worse, to compromise, the door to apprehension swings wide open: "Oh, things could have been different ..."

In contrast, satisficers are not haunted by their choices. Once they find an item that meets their standards, they stop looking. Moreover, they do not later agonize over what could have been.

Ironically, despite maximizers' quest for perfect product satisfaction and the glitz and flash that our consumer society bestows upon them, psychological research exposes these material overachievers as a miserable lot. It's true that their obsessive diligence often renders better choices – that is, as measured by objective standards of cost, quality, salary, and so on. But the cruel paradox is that these better choices produce less measurable contentment than the satisficers' approach of "Give it your best shot and get on with your life."

The greatest maximizers are the ones least happy with their outcomes. Their "doing better" offers scant pleasure, and when they take a wrong turn, their disappointment often morphs into self-torture. By psychological standards, maximizers' determination to make the best choice every time, every place has such a grip on them that they can rarely be at peace, and they accrue less contentment with life – less happiness, less cheerfulness. At worst, paramount maximizers border on clinical depression.

In fact, the maximizers our materialistic society adores are prime candidates for depression. The World Health Organization predicts that depression will soon become the number-two disease in the world, right behind heart disease. And a US government study published in the *Archives of General Psychiatry* reports that 45.8 percent of American university students harbor at least one psychological disorder, including obsessive, anti-social, and paranoid behaviors, along with drug and alcohol abuse.

At Columbia University, Rachel Elwork and Sheena Iyengar studied maximizer-type college seniors searching for jobs after graduation. Through their arduous foraging, these graduating students indeed found positions offering 20 percent higher starting salaries than the satisficer-type job seekers. Yet, despite the maximizers' greater monetary reward, their job-search ordeal brought them less satisfaction – indeed, it drained them to the point of utter exhaustion. Even more telling, once they were actually working their new job, they lost out to the satisficers in terms of overall job-satisfaction accrued.

Obviously, the research doesn't bode well for economic incentive and endeavor – or for those suffering from the contagious disease known as "affluenza."

◈ *Paying the Costs to Be the Boss* ◈

All this information pushes social researchers in general and behavioral economists in particular to question what's going on with *homo economicus,* the economically embroiled human being. The contemporary merging of economics and psychology into behavioral economics has generated profound insights into the material dynamics of human existence. It is intriguing that such research draws near tenets in ancient Krishna texts, such as the *Bhagavad-gita* and *Srimad-Bhagavatam*. Both clearly delineate mirages of material existence even more fundamental – and pathetic – than the maximizer/satisficer phenomenon.

"What is night for all beings," we read in the *Gita*, "is the time of awakening for the self-controlled; and the time of awakening for all beings is night for the introspective sage" (2.69). Here Krishna delineates social strata in a different way – neither by education nor by income, but by the focus of our senses and intelligence.

Attentive to the culture and habits of insight and enlightenment, the sage-like human being finds the "daytime" of the materially engrossed to be darkness. Meanwhile, what the knowledgeable spiritual adept considers the waking state, the dedicated materialist sees as unrealistic, impractical slumber.

Sleepwalking in the so-called daylight of organized,

external, bodily and mental affairs, the unfortunate addicts to material progress ignore their own true self-interest: spiritual development. In other words, from the viewpoint of a wisdom culture, the goal of steady economic expansion fails as a sufficient indicator of genuine human progress.

Sadly ignorant of spiritual dynamics, we plunge into the darkness and are pulled along by the waves of temporary happiness and distress, dreaming of how we can master, control, and enjoy. For as long as our bodies permit, we go for what we can, as much as we can. We live life – and ask questions later.

In contrast, the spiritual practitioner increasingly savors the spiritual sunshine of supramundane pleasure. The gradual progress of genuine culture elevates the spiritually astute out of the night of ignorance, above the rise and fall of material endeavors, to spiritual reality.

Deepening what the *Bhagavad-gita* bestows, *Srimad-Bhagavatam* further illuminates the paradoxes of existence: "In this temporary, material world, all materialists desire to achieve happiness and diminish their distress; therefore they act accordingly. Actually, however, we are happy as long as we do not endeavor for material happiness. As soon as we begin our plans for material happiness, mark it – this is where our conditions of distress begin" (7.7.42).

Dexterous use of the body, senses, wealth, and social connections for achieving all-embracing material gain and comfort is the goal propagated by an avaricious society (though most never attain it). The ancient yoga texts, particularly the *bhakti* writings, expose these goals as futile, life negating.

Current social-scientific research confirms that material endeavors have in-built problems yielding the happiness and satisfaction we expect. Even those who manage to achieve material success – as elusive and flickering as it is – miss the target of personal fulfillment they thought would accompany their acquisitions.

๏ *Opportunity Knocks – for a Price* ๏

The first barrier troubling the human material happiness industry is termed *opportunity costs*. We cannot properly assess the value of any choice we make if we consider it in isolation from the alternatives – the options that accompany any decision. Your choice to snowboard on New Zealand's South Island, for instance, precludes scuba diving on the North Island or flying over to Australia's Great Barrier Reef.

Especially for maximizers, the more options available, and the better they are, the more gnawing – after any choice – the sense of loss. Even the most attractive preference becomes devalued by the inevitable presence of alternatives. After you choose among various favorable prospects, the choice-outcomes will yield less satisfaction as you pay the price of opportunity: "I wonder what the other would have been like."

The alert maximizer, the consummate consumer, is conscious that every choice will cost. The toll for the roads not taken must be subtracted from the satisfaction-value of the final decision, the road chosen. Sometimes this puzzle, what Barry Schwartz terms "the paradox of choice," weighs so heavily that material lifestyle-maximizers "lock up," like a computer frozen mid-process.

Satisficers get by much more easily. They don't mind lowering the bar to something that is merely good. "I saw some possibilities," one might say, "and I made my selection. Good enough." With their lower anxieties from opportunity costs, they are happier in all respects.

But where in the world is the satisficer-type honored,

or even encouraged? Nations of *homo economicus* are addicted to endless economic growth at any cost – mental or physical, social or environmental. And who tabulates the spiritual price?

The compulsion for growth pushes people to constantly seek something better – a newer, faster, more customized version. Retailers beckon: "We have five hundred varieties of this, one thousand of that. Choose, choose, buy, buy, replace what you bought, add on to what you have – more, bigger, faster, better."

But what if the people en masse dared to diminish their consumption – were satisfied with a simple life and thereby reduced opportunity costs because of fewer material choices? What would happen?

Mainstream experts tell us that businesses and factories would close, sparking massive unemployment. Less tax revenue means that government coffers would dry up, social services wane. The United States might even reduce military spending. The world would become like Detroit or Greece – entire cities and nations tottering on the brink or plummeting over the edge.

✍ *Regret Increases the Rate* ✍

The second barrier blocking material satisfaction is "regret sensitivity." Besides the reality of a devalued choice, there is also the possibility that the choice we settle upon turns out to be a disaster: not only would scuba diving have been better than snowboarding, but the weather on the mountain unexpectedly warmed and the ski slope was literally a washout. Maximizers torture themselves with remorse: "What a mistake I made – what an idiot!"

Especially in the First World, the gospel prevails that

if we maximize to the utmost, we won't lament our decision down the road. You've got to make the perfect choice now – or bust! If a situation presents no alternatives, what can be done – but that's life in the Third World, right? Living in the developed world means that we're awash in a sea of options. Therefore we free-market consumer kings and queens must maximize unfailingly, to the nth degree.

Here we are greeted by another thorny paradox. Social scientists find that despite the regret-persecution that maximizers suffer, a major reason why individuals seek to become maximizers is precisely that: fear of a future regret. Illusioned, we think we must materially maximize – to avoid pain, shame, and regret. But when, inevitably, a maximized choice fails, we kick ourselves in the head.

To trigger the headache known as regret sensitivity, two factors combine. First, the more personal responsibility you feel for an outcome, the greater the guilt. And second, after your choice, the more you can envision a better alternative – what might have been – the greater the lamentation that follows.

❧ Where Did the Magic Go? ❧

Along with opportunity costs and regret sensitivity, a third barrier dulls our happiness, corrodes our satisfaction, and steals our fulfillment. Recent research by Daniel Gilbert of Harvard and Timothy Wilson of the University of Virginia focuses on *adaptation* – that when you do manage to get what you want, your struggle is not complete. Now you have to cope with diminishing returns.

This concept has been addressed for millennia by India's spiritual literature. As the *Bhagavad-gita* tells us, "Intelligent persons never participate in the sources of misery, which arise from the material senses interacting with temporary objects of gratification. Because these so-called pleasures have a beginning and an end, the wise do not seek to enjoy them" (5.22).

Let's say you decide to buy a Lexus. Once you get behind the wheel, you put all the other appealing car models out of your mind. You've chosen, and you've got it. Peace.

At first, Gilbert says, you feel great – *my* acquisition, *my* possession. The mind wraps around the new possession and absorbs it. But this equipoise is only temporary. Sooner or later – and generally more sooner than later – the freshness of your acquisition deteriorates and the whole "I've got my Lexus" experience starts to lose its fizz. Over time, adaptation takes over, and whatever apparent satisfaction you derived from your purchase fades.

Next, you're hit with a double punch. Adaptation – familiarity deflating satisfaction – combines with opportunity costs, regret for what you didn't choose. This is a universal material phenomenon. Irrespective of what you want, once you finally achieve it, the initially refreshing waters of satisfaction evaporate. Still, you try repeatedly, because your assumptions and habit-energy propel you forward on what Gilbert and other experts in the field call "the hedonic treadmill."

❧ *Help – I'm Slipping Back!* ❧

The pressure on our fragile psyche continues to mount. How has life become such a merciless taskmaster? Enter the curse of high expectations – "the higher their perch, the farther the fall." *The New York Times* and CBS News jointly surveyed teenagers, asking them to compare their life with what they felt their parents had experienced at their age.

Half the teenagers from affluent homes voiced an interesting perspective: their lives, they believed were harder.

Why so? Born with a silver spoon in their mouth, these kids received the benefit of parents who either climbed to the top of the economic ladder or themselves had parents who birthed them there. Further questioning revealed that the pressure and strain felt even by teenagers from prosperous households was caused by them bearing a heavy yoke: their own expectations combined with those of their parents.

Both India's ancient spiritual texts and the findings of behavioral economics agree that high material expectations, whatever their origin, almost guarantee that perceived material outcomes will come up short in terms of measured personal satisfaction and fulfillment.

The teenagers surveyed felt the burden of excessive options: in short, too much choice, and the fear of "mischoosing." One wrong move, one slip, and you fall under the pack, trampled by the sharp go-getters eager to surpass you.

In today's global economy, residents of the affluent world, especially in highly competitive societies like the United States, approach this with great fear. After all, First-Worlders must get more, improve their position, increase their assets and acquisitions. If nothing else, they must maintain the status quo; there is no question of diminishing, living with less, falling back.

If we want to get off the hedonic treadmill, we have to look at other possibilities for how to organize human beings and their economic affairs, other pathways for satisfying human needs and wants.

World history shows that while various political systems and leaders come and go, the minds of the people remain chronically out of control. Even prosperous nation-states cannot raise the bar of measured happiness beyond a basic and tenuous level. The inundation of materialistic choice and the resulting pressure to constantly select the best bring out the worst in an uncontrolled mind.

Spiritual Economics

I'm not advocating the kind of restriction of choice that we saw under state-enforced socialism. Having spent eight years organizing underground *bhakti-yoga* activities behind the Iron Curtain, I know first hand what life was like in the Soviet empire: pompous but poorly constructed mega-supermarkets with aisle upon aisle of shelves half-stocked with only one "brand" each of a limited range of items.

The free-market economies of today's democracies are different, but social researchers specializing in choice and abundance have concluded that in terms of measured happiness, these "advanced" political economies rest on deeply flawed assumptions. The materialistic dream that things will be better when as many humans as possible can dive into an ocean of material choices, goods, and lifestyles has failed. Careful social investigation demonstrates that beyond a modest level of option-availability and option-acquisition, people are not going to become any happier – indeed they can even become more distressed.

Srimad-Bhagavatam describes a five-year-old, exceptionally advanced child-yogi, Prahlada, appealing to his abnormally acquisitive, hedonistic father, a ferociously despotic head of state:

My dear father, please give up your depraved mind-set. End the discrimination in your heart between

enemies and friends; make your mind equipoised toward all. Know that except for the uncontrolled and
misguided mind, no enemy lurks within this world.
When we see everyone on the platform of equality,
we arrive on the best path to the Supreme. (7.8.9)

Imagining we have liberty and freedom, we suffer from our
only real enemy: our own mind. It bewilders and enslaves
us, concocting an illusory playground of artificial desires.
And then, when we are not ultimately happy, satisfied, we
blame others for our frustration.

Considering freedom from a social angle, Nobel-
laureate economist Amartya Sen of Harvard and Cam-
bridge provides a provocative and exhaustive analysis of the
link between freedom, choice, and economic expansion.
At the time of his Nobel Prize, in 1998, Sen was a rather
controversial pick, owing to his concentration on "welfare
economics" – his positing human welfare as central to economic thought. He dared to present human well-being as
the *goal,* not a side effect, of social and economic life.

Praised by the Nobel Committee for bringing both an
ethical framework and a moral authority to a field usually
dominated by technical specialists, Sen asserts that freedom necessitates more than quantities of choice, and that
sometimes too much choice both endangers freedom and
impedes economic and social development.

The research of David Myers, professor of psychology at
Hope College, and Robert E. Lane, Yale professor emeritus
of political science, likewise highlights the gap between our
material affluence and our well-being.

Myers studies the paradox of the American pre-
recession thirty-year economic soar and its accompanying
socio-psychological drop. As incomes and consumer prod-
ucts doubled, down went happiness, community spirit, and

job security, and up went crime, fractured relationships, demoralized children, and depression.

In his study of free-market democracies, Lane, like Myers, identifies materialism and disproportionate individualism as the prime offenders. But he also points to ways by which our free-market fetishism – indeed, our whole economic system – has undermined our happiness.

Lane, who has served as president of both the American Political Science Organization and the International Society of Political Psychology, is certainly not "anti-free enterprise." He does insist, however, that the market and democracy left on their own do not necessarily generate increased well-being.

Social statistics effectively lay to rest the passionate belief that in the developed world, increasing the GDP increases happiness. In the past decade, a profusion of research on North America, Europe, and Japan has punctured that unsubstantiated notion, labeled by Lane as the "Economistic Fallacy," which he deems to be a major threat to the future of the First World.

Lane's recommendation? When devising policies, governments should ask if the policies contribute to three main goals: happiness, justice, and personal development.

Richard Layard, emeritus professor at the London School of Economics, also urges that we heed the data that reveals the Economistic Fallacy. Founder of Europe's leading economics research center, Layard urges us not to hide from the evidence that the average person today is no happier than the average person fifty years ago – in spite of incomes more than doubling and consumer goods proliferating.

Paul Hawken, writer, co-founder of the Smith & Hawken garden-tools company, and a main force in the sustainability movement, encapsulates our imprudence in a profound way: "We have an economy where we steal the future, sell it in the present, and call it GDP."

Again, in *Srimad-Bhagavatam*, Prahlada, speaks to his demon of a father:

> Throughout the history of the world lived many fools like you who did not conquer the six enemies. These six foes, the mind and five senses, plunder the wealth of the human body. Excessively proud fools with uncontrolled mind and senses assume, "I have nullified the opposition in every direction, whether at home or abroad." But if a person conquers the six enemies within and shows equipoise toward all living entities, such a saintly sage has no actual foes to contend with. Owing to residual ignorance, a person's own illusions fabricate opposition. (7.8.10)

In the name of freedom, prosperity, and progress, our political economies sponsor the citizenry's unbridled minds and senses. The people's resultant wildness within then diverts whatever power of focus their short lifetimes provide to false problems and solutions.

❧ *Where to Next?* ❧

We must face the music: we've reached a point in history where we must rethink the very nature and meaning of human progress. Rather than becoming our economic deliverance and staircase of increasing social well-being, the creed of mass-marketing and ceaseless consumption has shown itself to be a charade. Humanity can't handle the burden on its psyche, and nature can't handle the burden on its biosphere. It is now legitimate both in the academy and the media to question the hopes, beliefs, and dreams that have become a sinkhole.

We need a new vision of society, a new revelation of economics that is not torpedoed by the myth of constant growth or plagued by the paradoxes of choice and abundance. With increased and increasing depression and substance abuse, societies in the First World dangle the possibility of "the good life," manifested in stylish clothes, luxury cars, oversized housing, overseas traveling, and food from every region of the world. But whether or not they attain The Dream, the average Joe and Jane are no happier than before. In the Third World, a rise of income in abysmal conditions does increase the level of measured material happiness, but only up to a basic middle-class standard. Then the benefit halts.

We can analyze, critique, and lament our lot, but what about constructing a new vision, a better social blueprint? Our socio-economic crisis in happiness is actually an identity crisis. To formulate a genuine and effective alternative, we require an alternative way of understanding *who* we are – *what* we are.

❧ Beyond Matter-Mania ❧

We engage in economic activities to satisfy our needs and wants. Obviously then, we have to understand who and what we are, so that we may understand our actual needs and wants, and work to fulfill them. According to the Western materialistic economic perspective, human beings are nothing more than producing-consuming machines of matter, whose best interests are realized when production and consumption perform at peak efficiency.

In contrast, the Krishna texts of India's yogic tradition

of spiritual knowledge reveal that human beings are multidimensional entities, whose wants and needs can't be analyzed solely in terms of one limited dimension.

If we are simply the body, *just* matter, then there *might* be some validity to exclusively materialistic economics; matter and our quest for it could be the totality of our short life in a purposeless universe, randomly formed from fluctuations of nothingness that, in turn, begot chance matter interactions. But if we are something more than matter – if we have another dimension to our self and the universe has an in-built purpose – then our quest for fulfillment and satisfaction has to proceed in a different direction.

Consciousness is the symptom of our spiritual nucleus. There is no provable material explanation of consciousness, and it cannot be measured or even detected by any scientific instrument. In fact, the only material reason we have to assume consciousness in others is because we know it in ourselves. Based on that firsthand evidence of my own consciousness, I think that you're also conscious – because you're acting and feeling like me. But there is no direct scientific evidence of my being conscious, of your being conscious, or of what consciousness actually is.

Scientists who comment on consciousness tend to fall into three groups. One bloc says, "We don't know now, but we hope to know in the future." The second asserts, "Consciousness is matter; it's a purely neurochemical phenomenon. Though we can't say exactly what consciousness is, we all know it has to be physical – like everything else in existence." And the third bloc says, "We don't know what consciousness is, and we'll probably never know – it will always elude the reach of science as we know it."

There you have it, the state of the art about what should be the most important field of human inquiry. Without understanding our consciousness, how can we say we truly understand economics, science, or anything, since everything comes to us through the medium of our consciousness?

Some people may object, "Oh, here we go again – the ghost in the machine. You're advocating some kind of phantom in the body – vitalism. How quaint." But let's flip that bias. Via the mechanism of the unknown – consciousness – you're trying to establish the known. And through the unknown, you're trying to perceive the known. At issue is not the ghost in the machine – *it's the machine in the ghost!*

❧ *Lost Identity* ❧

If we can understand the actual make-up of the human being, we can then construct our socio-economics on a platform that features a sane, more satisfying way of life. One may inquire, "If our consciousness indicates a spiritual reality, how is it that we've forgotten it?" The Krishna texts state that owing to our modus operandi of interacting with matter according to an exploitative, manipulative, domineering agenda, we suffer loss of our spiritual vision and understanding.

Consequently, as the resultant material immersion increases, the ABCs of spiritual knowledge, taught by Krishna at the start of the *Bhagavad-gita*, seem far beyond our comprehension:

> As you, the nonmaterial particle within the body, continuously traverse from childhood to youth to old age, similarly, at death your real self transfers to another body. This change does not bewilder a truly sensible, level-headed person. (2.13)

Our false identification with matter as the self and material gratification as a goal is no inconsequential affair. Such a decisive error produces forgetfulness of our spiritual identity and absorption in a temporary, artificial identity. Misidentification of the self as matter is step one, and step two is that this false identification with matter spawns a concocted attitude of masterfulness in relation to our body and this world.

Again, *Srimad-Bhagavatam* expands upon our predicament. The sobering question is raised:

> Generally human beings discern that their attempts for gratifying the senses award them many dismal ordeals. Yet still they try to enjoy. O Krishna, despite their accumulated knowledge, how can they proceed to act just like a dog, an ass or a goat? (11.8.8)

Krishna elucidates upon this riddle of existence:

> Intelligence lost, a person first falsely identifies the self with the material body and mind. As such deceptive knowledge arises within the consciousness, material passion, the cause of great suffering, pervades the mind, displacing its original goodness. The mind, now contaminated by passion, plunges into making and changing many ideas and plans for material advancement. In this way, a foolish person, constantly meditating on material nature, accumulates unbearable material desires. (*Srimad-Bhagavatam* 11.8.9–10)

Once society en masse swallows the pill of identifying the body of matter as the self, socio-economic muddle and eventual mayhem prevail – though the dysfunctionalism is structured and marketed to us as the developed First World. The complexity and severity of life's problems multiply according to how deep the illusion of matter-misidentification cuts.

❧ Krishna Knows the Business Cycle ❧

The *Bhagavad-gita* provides us with a clear analysis that fingers the root of the mass consumerism we honor as "progress." Highlighting our mind's preoccupations that morph into obsessions and then impel our senses, Krishna explains the process of material illusion and entanglement in the mesh of material nature. While contemplating the objects of the senses, He says, a person develops attachment for these sensory targets.

This mental bonding, of course, is every marketer's dream: "They're envisioning my product – it's entered their mind. Soon they'll feel attachment for it – a hidden emotional connection – and the product becomes them." When – or if – the consumer wakes up to the futility of his or her position, the marketer is nowhere to be found. As top Wall Street movers and shakers intoned in the years leading up to the 2008 banking crisis, "IBG/YBG" – I'll be gone; you'll be gone. Before the public caught on, the financial schemers had made off with their plunder.

Such attachment, Krishna describes, generates a robust desire, a deep-set yearning, a *lust*, for interacting with that object. Implanted in the mind is the conviction that attaining the desired object will generate a worthwhile portion of fulfillment. And just as people acquire and discard consumer goods, they also pick up and drop personal relationships, "hooking up" in serial affairs.

Material life is all about desire. Subtly or explicitly, we lust. Items, situations, relationships, attitudes – we hanker to possess, control, and enjoy them. Therefore we'll agree

63

to material life's daily grind, accepting the competitive toil as necessary – "the real world."

What's the beginning of this business cycle? It starts with contemplation: "Ooh yes, I need it; I want it; that'll satisfy me." This meditation is followed by the struggle of material existence. Attachment ripens into lust, which we'll do almost anything to satisfy: "Yes, I agree to undergo ordeals, dramas, and hustles just to fulfill my desires."

Krishna states that next, the frustration of our desires leads to anger. All material desires, drummed into our consciousness, result in internal discontentment and disquiet, which then transforms to anger – whether seething within or bursting without. The desire to enjoy the material world and its affairs cannot award the inner satisfaction and fulfillment the real self needs. Therefore we both inherit and bestow the legacy of perpetual material unrest:

> While dwelling upon the objects of the senses, a person develops attachment to them. From such attachment arises lust, selfish desire. That craving then breeds anger.
>
> From anger, confusion follows. This complete misapprehension leads to disruption of our memory bank of crucial life-understanding. When that memory is bewildered, intelligence, vital discrimination, is lost. Upon our losing such intelligence, we sink, lost in the material mire. (*Bhagavad-gita* 2.62–63)

Some people may shrink from the *Gita's* presentation of this desire chain, adjudge the analysis too spiritually "gooey" for any practical application in today's aggressive urban jungles and fading rural communities. But there is also a predominance of cutting-edge research by prominent academics revealing the drawbacks of too much materialistic choice, the cost of opportunity, the onset of regret sensitivity, and the downside of high expectations.

We've heard enough for even the narrow-minded to consider that the ancient knowledge in the Krishna texts is looking increasingly contemporary and frontline.

Economic issues and affairs rule the day. But our understanding of economics has no spiritual foundation. It is no wonder that ever-escalating lust, avarice, stress, and depression have become society's taskmasters.

When society as a whole neglects the cultivation of higher qualities, what better outcome can we expect? Albert Einstein is credited with saying that a problem is never solved on its own level, on the same level that spawned it. Human crises, whether individual or mass, are never resolved with the same consciousness that created them.

❧ *Every Social Body Needs a Brain* ❧

The beginning of *Srimad-Bhagavatam* places us in the midst of a symposium held thousands of years ago. Attending the event were the greatest sages, mystics, and meditators of ancient India's yogic civilization. The place, named Naimisharanya, can still be found today, near the city of Lucknow in northern India.

The illustrious participants gathered with the determination that none would leave until they could understand what was the absolute and ultimate good for all people. With their psychic vision, these sadhus could look ahead into the coming millennia. What they saw profoundly concerned them.

Human beings, they envisioned, would become increasingly disrupted in their ability to focus on spiritual knowledge and applied wisdom. Their minds shackled to short-term ambitions, their natural lucidity and self-control disrupted by the weapons of mass distraction, overloaded by fleeting psycho-physical stimuli, they would squander the precious gift of human consciousness on immediate profits and lusty gratifications, neglecting their prime duty to understand the ultimate goal and good.

For the minority who would seek to perfect their life, the assembled spiritual scientists detected a major hurdle. The general population would perceive a profusion of spiritual literatures advocating diverse remedies, a multitude of spiritual saints offering assorted advice.

Sympathizing that people would not be able to sort through the intricacies of the vast metaphysical science, the mystic philosophers accepted the mission of clarifying and codifying the essence of all good advice, for the total benefit of all living beings. Scanning the spiritual heritage of their advanced wisdom-culture, the erudite sages united to formulate a solution.

The theme of this compassionate convention was how the true self, meaning the nonmaterial entity, could attain genuine fulfillment and satisfaction. Following timeless yoga etiquette, the sages submitted this question to the most senior, adept spiritual consultant in their midst, Suta Goswami. His Sanskrit title, *goswami*, means "master of the mind and senses."

Suta Goswami responded:

Assembled sadhus, O fellow spiritual academics, I've been appropriately questioned by you. Your questions are commendable because they relate to the Complete Whole, Krishna, and are therefore relevant to the full welfare of the entire world. Yours is the only type of inquiry that leads to comprehensive satisfaction of the self. (*Srimad-Bhagavatam* 1.2.5)

The Sanskrit word for self is *atma*. Depending on context, it can refer to any three levels of a multidimensional living being: body, mind, and core spirit-self. The explicit, governing premise, however, is that these three dimensions are not equal – in duration, value, or importance.

At the lowest level, *atma* refers to the body; at the medium, the mind; and at its deepest and most significant level, what is essential, our spiritual core, what does not change, even as the body and mind do. In Chapter 2 of the *Bhagavad-gita*, Krishna relates the changing body and mind to changes of clothing:

> Just as a person acquires new garments, discarding worn-out ones, similarly the nonmaterial self, the *atma,* enters new material bodies, discarding the old and useless ones. (2.22)

Although we are not our clothes, we take care of them; likewise, though the body and mind are temporary casings, we maintain them as well as possible, to the best of our ability. The symposium of sadhus, headed by Suta Goswami, knew that the first priority of humanity is to cultivate the essence, the nonmaterial core, the spirit-self. With this vital spotlight beaming, the sages began to analyze human economic affairs.

❧ *"They Say the Best Things in Life Are Free, But ..."* ❧

There is an old saying: "Life's real pleasure is not taking but giving." It is a simple platitude, but Suta Goswami and the sadhus of Naimisharanya expanded it far beyond common, mundane experience.

Our economic structures have made the natural pleasure

of giving difficult to perform. A few donations to charity notwithstanding, our overriding emphasis is on acquisition. To satisfy yourself, you must *get*. We all have wants – whether lukewarm red-hot – that seem to have converted into needs, which we feel we must meet, and never neglect. The more affluence you can amass, the more choices – pathways to satisfaction – arrive at your door or inbox.

To buck this social tide requires great motivation and perseverance. Lacking the requisite momentum, we'll fail to escape the individual and societal patterns of "business as usual." But from where will that impetus spring? Transforming an economy of *taking* into an economy of *giving* necessitates tapping into higher awareness and energies. Only the development of spiritual knowledge and values will empower people and society to make the crucial saner choices.

Defining the higher ground of being, Suta Goswami and the sages established that all the occupational activities of human society are actually meant to bring about enlightenment, freedom from illusion. Human beings, they emphasized, should never work simply for material gain:

> All occupational undertakings should have the eventual purpose of spiritual advancement. Material gain should not be the end-goal. Moreover, previous great sages have already delineated that those working in the best occupation – fulltime pursuance of enlightenment – should never resort to material gain for achieving sense indulgence. (*Srimad-Bhagavatam* 1.2.9)

This is the profound adjustment that can turn around our economic ship. The Krishna texts are pointing out that instead of socio-economic affairs draining human beings of their essential higher aspirations in life, the daily activities of society can function in a way that elevates humanity.

Few people would go to their jobs without remuneration. What we are learning here, though, is that while economic affairs produce at least some degree of material reward, this gain should not be considered the preeminent fruit of our labor. Additionally, the sages issued a directive to the spiritual specialists, those exceptional persons whose sole and full occupation is inner development. Their life dedicated to aiding the spiritual progress of others, they must never pursue material profit for material gratification.

For the benefit of the general population and its leaders, present and future, Suta Goswami continues:

> Desires, the thrust of life, should never center upon sense gratification. One should desire only a healthy life, sustenance, because the human form is especially meant for inquiry into the Supreme Truth. Work should have no other goal. (*Srimad-Bhagavatam* 1.2.10)

❧ *Yoga as the Art of Work* ❧

The Krishna texts urge us to execute our tasks to attain spiritual development through the workplace, through legitimate occupational duties. Go to work so you can give – not so you can get.

Regardless of income level, this inspiring spiritual mentality of munificence begins with our constant meditation on how the fruits of our labor – our money earned – can facilitate a spiritual lifestyle.

Meditate on this. How can the proceeds from your work directly serve to deepen your spiritual experience and spiritual knowledge? After all, every individual's first duty is how he or she can escape illusion and progress toward spiritual enlightenment. Then you can effectively consider how to help others spiritually advance. If you have a family, your career contemplation extends beyond yourself: how the money you earn can facilitate *their* spiritual advancement.

Whether or not you have a family, you can meditate on how your work can expedite the spiritual development of as many people as your earnings allow. A proper wisdom culture holds that all human beings, even all creatures, are members of the same family. Krishna says, "Understand that all species of life, regardless of bodily form, eventuate by birth from material nature, and I am the seed-giving father" (*Bhagavad-gita* 14.4).

Are you constrained by tight finances? The key is that low income, high income, or shrinking middle, we offer all we honestly can, for the spiritualization of our own life and for the global family. If you are profiting in the millions, think big: use your occupation to enable the spiritual education and experience for an entire city or nation.

This spiritualized economy of giving, not getting – though intriguing – may seem to bear the weighty baggage of religious belief. I empathize with these possible jitters – religious fundamentalism has put us all on guard. We have to move beyond "religion," beyond belief, to actual spiritual experience. Comprehensive spiritual knowledge can deliver that. Far beyond the disputations of religious belief, the techniques for authentic spiritual experience, described in the Krishna texts, have the potency to renovate our sensory interactions.

If we introduce this spiritual technology to people, their internal dynamics will be transformed. They will develop the vision and vigor to look upon their work as a portal to spiritual development. Occupations are certainly necessary for sustaining the body, but the over-arching goal of work should be how to increase the general stock of spiritual enlightenment, for the individual and for society.

Krishna describes yoga as the consummate expertise in all fields of endeavor, the greatest skillfulness in action. "Therefore strive for yoga," He directs, "which is the art of all work" (*Bhagavad-gita* 2.50).

"In all circumstances of life, be a yogi" (6.46).

Increasingly, yoga-fitness practitioners are grasping that the term *yoga* does not simply refer to the world's best system of exercises for the body and breath. The texts of devotional yoga, *bhakti-yoga*, such as the *Gita* and *Srimad-Bhagavatam*, describe yoga as linking all human endeavors, including economic affairs, to the ultimate source of all energies: Krishna. *Krishna* means the unlimitedly attractive source, the Complete Conscious Whole, from which both matter and spirit emanate. The cream of yogic knowledge proclaims that understanding Krishna is the paramount mission in human life.

∾ *Up from Illusion* ∾

If profound, extensive spiritual wisdom can provide us with the spiritual technology for yoking our occupational experience to the Ultimate Source, and if we can distribute that nonmaterial experience to others, we run no risk from the maladies of inner deterioration and breakdown. We bypass the paradoxical psychological costs of affluence, choice, and acquisition.

Instead of selfishly cultivating material motivations that never fulfill the real self, an enlightened workforce would tap into the best wellspring of incentive: the prosperity of contributing to the nonmaterial, permanent individual, family, and societal self. "I'm going to work to give – facilitating advancement in spiritual knowledge, technique, and culture for me, my family, and as much of society as possible.

71

Beyond the temporary material body, mind, and senses covering us, what will attract and satisfy the *atma,* the real self, the spirit soul? Spiritual knowledge and experience will do that, not our clinging to external, material labels of gender, ethnicity, nationality, or creed.

The same maximizer syndrome that drains us materially can benefit us when applied spiritually. The sages gathered for the symposium at Naimisharanya show us how. Once we know that the goal of human life is to obtain the most profound and comprehensive spiritual knowledge possible, we can truly "get down to business." Surveying the spiritual marketplace, analyzing the options, checking the reviews, sifting, discussing, and studying, we do our homework – we want the deepest and most inclusive answers to all questions about the self, existence, and ultimate reality.

When that maximizer consciousness is applied to consumption, personal troubles multiply. But take that same attitude and apply it to the quest for comprehensive spiritual knowledge, and the maximizer does great. The purity of consciousness advocated in Krishna texts can supply what we so desperately need: vast spiritual knowledge combined with tools for precise spiritual experience. Krishna, the Supreme Fulfiller of Desire, gives us full assurance:

> Because you are never envious of Me, I shall convey to you this most confidential knowledge and practical realization. Know it and be free from the miseries of material existence.
>
> This *bhakti* knowledge is the king of education, the most secret of all secrets. It is the purest knowledge, and because it gives direct perception of the self by realization, you can directly experience the results. It is the perfection of dharma, everlasting, and joyfully practiced. (*Bhagavad-gita* 9.1–2)

A sane and beneficial human society awards access to superior levels of fulfillment. Benign governments, seeking
the all-embracing welfare of the people, will serve to expedite society's nonsectarian innermost needs. This is a real
stimulus package. Once the freeways to higher, spiritual
fulfillment are open, only then will we see diminishment of
the enemies within – the negative qualities and ambitions
devastating the individual and the planet.

*Spiritual
Economics*

The *giving* economy is a solution that won't happen
based on moral platitudes, religious beliefs, or socio-
political adjustments. We can talk about social, political,
and economic change until we're blue in the face, but unless people can access the superior pleasure of the real self,
they'll never extricate themselves from the inner and outer
destructiveness wrought by *homo economicus.*

The most profound economic implications of the ancient yoga information are that we have something else
about us that we must nourish. Krishna points out what
should be on the table, and how we fail by not obtaining it:

> The embodied self may seek to restrict the senses,
> but the taste for interacting with material sense ob-
> jects – the thirst for the inferior – stubbornly per-
> sists. If, however, the spiritual seeker drops material
> gratifications because of savoring the supreme flavor,
> then such a *bhakti* practitioner can remain fixed in
> transcendental consciousness. (*Bhagavad-gita* 2.59)

This higher taste, superior flavor, is not theoretical or be-
lief-ish. It is the authentic experience, by purified senses, of
a superior, nonmaterial reality of relationship – the Love
Supreme.

Are we just matter engaged in a cycle of production and consumption? Comprehending consciousness as the product of matter is a neuroscience dead-end. The failure of "neuromania," seeing the brain as the only vehicle of understanding, tips us off to the nonmaterial dimension of the self and reality.

Once we accept the necessity of nonmaterial means of satisfaction, we can look at economic activity with a refreshingly different vision. We'll see an extraordinary transformation in society only when people understand that all the affairs of humanity, especially economics, are meant to culminate in spiritual enlightenment. As long as the predominant culture promotes as foremost our temporary body and senses – and all the objects and entities temporarily desired by and allied with them – enduring peace and harmony will elude us. Such a misguided societal and global atmosphere will guarantee humanity maximum obstruction in pondering the authentic purpose of our human body and its role in the universe.

The time to consider crucial points of human purpose is now. Countless experts tell us that human economic and environmental affairs can't continue as they are. But our institutions, and the humans that perpetuate them, are gridlocked and baffled – unable to alter course.

Just as the yogic sages of antiquity recognized, the root issues demand our attention. Only then can we comprehend beneficial economic affairs.

What is the *atma*; what is the self? And beyond even the *atma*, the spirit-soul, that finite unit of consciousness, there is also the supreme *atma*, the infinite conscious entity, who includes and facilitates all the minute particle-units of consciousness. The link-up between the *atma* and what is termed in Sanskrit the *Paramatma*, the supreme *atma*, generates the real, ever-increasing pleasure of life.

How to maximize the nonmaterial personal relationship between the living beings (the finite particles of spiritual consciousness) and the infinite, the superconscious source – this is what *bhakti*, Krishna consciousness, is all about. Mining that relationship between the individual soul and Krishna, the supreme soul, yields spiritual pleasure incomparable to the temporary gross and subtle gratifications of material existence.

By educating the population in the knowledge and technology for accessing what is inexhaustible and unrestricted by time and space, the political and economic leaders of the world can steer society to lasting benefit. Krishna invites us to contemplate, desire, and interact with the spiritual product. Applied spiritual knowledge, resulting in spiritual experience, will protect human society from destructively selfish, lower drives – while nourishing the genuine needs of the real self. Only then can we build a sane future.

CHAPTER SIX

Eluding the Matrix of Illusion

*Expanded from a presentation given at
Stanford University in March 2012.*

What does it mean to be truly awake? Perhaps we are just sleepwalking through the day after slumbering more deeply at night? Lost in a simulation, a massively staged virtual reality, we all might be undergoing a high-tech version of Plato's "Allegory of the Cave."

Chained inside a cavern, Plato's victims pass their time spellbound, staring at silhouetted shapes flickering on a wall. Unknown to the enthralled prisoners, the captivating show originates behind them, at the cave's entrance, where light from a fire casts shadows of various objects. Perceiving these shadows as essential substance, the bewildered bunch, representative of human society, never pierce the veil. Mesmerized, they continuously gaze at the shadows – what they accept as reality. They will never know the real objects, so inadequately represented by the shadows consuming their life.

The sci-fi classic *The Matrix* leaves its audience to puzzle over whether they can know what is real, what is not, and what is our relationship to reality. Depicting a dystopia in which a simulated reality called the matrix imprisons humans, the film successfully destabilizes viewers, prompting them, at least for a night, to call into question the foundational assumptions of their existence.

In his book *Philosophers Explore The Matrix,* author Christopher Grau elaborates: "A viewer of *The Matrix* is naturally led to wonder: how do I know I am not in the matrix? How do I know for sure that my world is not also a sophisticated charade, put forward by some superhuman intelligence in such a way that I could not possibly detect the ruse?"

When Morpheus, the rescuer and reality trainer, mercifully deprograms Neo, the film's hero, he dispels all Neo's illusions:

MORPHEUS: Have you ever had a dream, Neo, that you were so sure was real? What if you were unable to wake from that dream? How would you know the difference between the dream world and the real world? The matrix is everywhere. It is all around us. Even now, in this very room. You can see it when you look out your window or when you turn on your television. You can feel it when you go to work ... when you go to church ... when you pay your taxes. It is the world that has been pulled over your eyes to blind you from the truth.

NEO: What truth?

MORPHEUS: That you are a slave, Neo. Like everyone else, you were born into bondage. Into a prison that you cannot taste or see or touch. A prison for your mind.

❧ *Night Dream, Daydream* ❧

The *Bhagavad-gita* introduces the perplexity of the real and the unreal straightaway. In Chapter 2, Krishna, identified in the *Gita* as the supreme instructor of yoga as well as its ultimate goal, explains for our welfare, "Seers of the truth have concluded that in the nonexistent, the impermanent, one finds no real being-ness. And in the existent, the permanent, one will never encounter nonbeing-ness. This the sages have concluded by studying both" (2.16).

From the yogic standpoint of applied spiritual technology, the terms *existent* and *nonexistent* refer to nonmatter and matter. And what is impermanent – in that sense, *nonexistent* – should not grab our major attention in life.

When seen from the viewpoint of eternity, the impermanent, like a blip on a radar screen, appears and vanishes almost instantly. Compared to the timeless, the nonmaterial, it is indeed nonexistent.

Clouds in the sky form, then disintegrate. Meanwhile, the sky remains. What sticks around is truly *existent.* Knowing the real standard of *existent*, spiritually advanced sages focus on what endures – the eternal.

Whether we are concerned with self-identity, energy, the cosmos, or the source of it all, our knowledge and lifestyles should tap into what abides, while everything else is changing, beginning, ending.

In line with the Vedic tradition of spiritual knowledge, the *Gita* lucidly advocates that first the scientific yogi should pierce the veil preventing us from discerning what is the nonexistent and existent self: the temporary, material self and the unending identity that lives on. Next, you can take on the world – what is stagecraft on a cosmic scale and why it is so.

The *Vedas* explain that the way we perceive the world depends on our state of consciousness, our level of awareness. We are, after all, dealing with appearances – the effects of something upon our consciousness. That something itself is unknown to us because of the filtration done by our senses, combined with the mediation done by our state of consciousness.

If we have not masterfully understood consciousness, what do we really know?

Directly perceived by any human, whether scientist or layperson, are only consciously experienced appearances, qualia, based on inputs of sensory data and their interrelationships. Regardless of our erudition, can we rely upon these phenomena and the hypothesized relationships between them, without comprehensively understanding consciousness itself – the medium of the message?

The answer comes to us when the alarm clock rings in the morning. While sleeping, we experience vivid dreams filled with what we accept, albeit in our sleep, as independently existing physical objects. We cavort with obliging lovers and fight off horrible attackers. But when the alarm sounds, the dreamtime world suddenly disappears and our consciousness enters the state of wakefulness. *Srimad-Bhagavatam* explains:

> While we sleep deeply, we dream and see in ourselves many other objects nearby, such as mountains, rivers, forests, snakes, horses, or perhaps even the entire universe, although they are actually far away. Upon awakening from a dream, sometimes we see that we are in a human form, lying in bed in one place. Then we see ourselves in terms of various conditions: a member of a particular family, ethnicity, class, occupation, ideology, creed, and so on. The phases of deep sleep, dreaming and wakefulness – also conditions – are just energies of the Supreme. One should always remember the originator of all these conditions, the Ultimate Source, who though producing the setup and its effects, is unaffected by them. (6.16.54)

How do we understand the perceptions we have while sleeping? It's not by how they look. The objects and people that populate our dreamworld appear to us as true as the components of our wakeful world.

We judge the difference by duration. Dream stuff vanishes when our sleep breaks. Awake stuff – though we may sometimes forget about it when we sleep – persists day after day, greets us when we rise from sleep. But awake stuff also vanishes with time.

Vedic teachers describe that the moment of death is very much like the moment a dream breaks. Hence, it seems that all we can honestly say is that some dreams last for a night, some for a day, and some for a lifetime. How, then, can we ever consider night-dream *or* daydream perceptions as bedrock truths of existence?

The genuine spiritual adept abandons the micro-illusion of thinking we are matter. Essential education begins when we give up the delusion that the body is the self. When we are freed from that mirage, we can then proceed further, to comprehend both what is this world and how we can cope with an impermanence that only seems to exist – the cosmic macro-illusion that comes and goes.

In *The Matrix,* the all-encompassing simulation, or more precisely the artificial intelligence running it, recalls shades of the seventeenth-century French philosopher Descartes. He proposed the "evil demon" hypothesis – that the world we perceive might actually be a mere illusion.

The *Bhagavad-gita* also discloses a grand cosmic deception, but one meant for our benefit. Krishna, speaking as the ultimate source of all phenomena, speaks frankly to strengthen potential candidates for enlightenment:

My energy of material illusion that bewilders living beings is extraordinarily difficult to overcome. But if you adopt My methodology, execute My way, then you can easily see your way through it. (*Bhagavad-gita* 7.14)

And in *Srimad-Bhagavatam*, we find more:

Know me to be the Supreme Absolute, the omnipresent Supreme Soul, through whom the sleeping living beings can understand their dreaming condition as well as their real happiness, beyond the activities of the material senses and environment. I am the cause of the activities of the sleeping living being. (6.16.55)

We all know it's difficult to admit that we may be lost in play-acting, absorbed in the make-believe of both the nightdream and the daydream. Defensively, we counter, "What do you mean *delusion, illusion, confusion*? My life is working out, and my material affairs are moving along. Who says I have to sort out all of existence? Why can't I just *be*?"

Our predominant belief is "one body, one opportunity, one lifetime," or, as Mae West said, "You only live once, but if you do it right, once is enough."

❧ *Lady, Sir – Can You Spare a Crisis?* ❧

Owing to our attachment to ongoing self-tranquilization, we may more readily spot our individual dilemmas on the micro level if we first examine our wider contexts, surveying human crises at the macro level.

"May you live in interesting times." This popular blessing often attributed to ancient Confucian China is, unknown to many, actually a curse, meaning "May you experience much disorder and commotion in your life." Moreover, its origin is Western and twentieth century.

Robert Kennedy publicized the phrase when addressing the University of Cape Town in 1966: "There is a Chinese curse which says 'May he live in interesting times.' Like it or not, we live in interesting times. They are times of danger and uncertainty; but they are also more open to the creative energy of men than any other time in history."

Two centuries ago, if somehow you could have seen the earth from outer space, you would have observed only two concentrations of glowing light, indicating populations over one million – coming from London and Beijing. Now, gazing from space, you would see at least 450 of these bright spots.

Every year, the equivalent of seven New Yorks is added to the world's population. By midcentury, the likes of two Chinas will swell the number to a projected nine billion. But what will be the quality of their lives? From where will nine billion human beings derive their resources, and where will they sink the resultant wastes? Some environmental researchers calculate that we are already living as if we were on at least one and a half planet Earths. And now we want to travel to other planets and trash them too.

We have a bumper crop of challenges. Former US Secretary of State Henry Kissinger quipped, "There cannot be a crisis next week. My schedule is already full."

Ecological woes, pandemics, population growth, nuclear proliferation, food shortages, water scarcity, conflict in the Middle East, a faltering global economy, a renewed cold war, wealth inequality – crises abound.

Our greatest challenge, however – the elephant in the room – is that our current institutions can't solve any of these challenges. Humanity's foremost crisis is institutional failure. Not only do our institutions fall flat at resolving our mega crises; they can't even prioritize them.

Select just one daunting issue – say, climate change. Is it

just a problem for science? No, or at least, not only; we're actually dealing with a triad of political, economic, and social cans of worms. The bottom line that the environmental predicament shares with other twenty-first-century problems is dysfunctional human behavior.

On both the individual and social level, we are plagued by dysfunctional lifestyles, practices, and policies. Consequently, many environmental strategists have realized that they must shift their primary emphasis from biophysical sciences to social sciences – a broad-spectrum approach focusing on our membership in a malignant society. Only then can we have any hope of meeting the multi-faceted threats of global warming or any of our other hydra-headed problems. The challenges are interrelated, entwined, as human issues – outgrowths of human dysfunction.

How can we escape the grip of an illusion so widespread and collective – this *mass consensual trance?*

The late, preeminent Stanford University climatologist Stephen Snyder posed an astute and penetrating question: "Can democracy survive complexity?" Looking ahead only as far as the next election or financial quarter, our much-vaunted Western institutions have lost even the semblance of long-term vision for what is the ultimate good and how to attain it.

Our current challenges are so interrelated, interlocked, and multidisciplinary that we have to view them holistically. Vedic wisdom tells us that an effective holistic approach must include not only human beings, not even only all living beings – the parts – but also the Complete Whole, supremely conscious, existing in and of itself and for itself, greater than the sum of its parts. The Vedic text *Sri Isopanishad*, an Upanishad specializing in knowledge of ultimate proprietorship, elaborates:

84

The Supreme Absolute Truth is perfect and complete, and because He is completely perfect, all emanations from Him, such as even this perceivable world, are perfectly equipped as complete wholes. Whatever is produced of the Complete Whole is also complete in itself. Because He is the Complete Whole, even though so many complete units emanate from Him, He remains the complete balance. (Invocation)

The *Bhagavad-gita*, which is also known as the *Gitopanishad* – the cream of all the Upanishads – expands on this. As the *Gita* unfolds, we witness an individual, Arjuna, being acutely challenged. When the individual is wobbly, institutional ineffectiveness will automatically follow, since institutions derive from individuals. Improving institutional capacity to make better decisions that do not jeopardize human survival means improving the stock of human wisdom, individually and collectively. A wisdom culture is our greatest need.

To varying degrees, individuals act in a society collectively, as co-creators and participants – or as some say, as co-deluders and the deluded. So if we focus on how human beings perform as individuals, we can see the root cause of institutional challenges.

❧ The Yoga of Crisis ❧

In 2004, referring to the competition that America faced from rapidly rising education levels in other nations, Stanford economist Paul Romer coined the saying "A crisis is a terrible thing to waste." Now at New York University's Stern School of Business, he heard an echo of his crisis mantra in 2008, when President Obama's chief of staff invoked it at the beginning of the global financial meltdown.

The *Bhagavad-gita* builds upon this maxim. Its first pages place us at the epicenter of a huge, escalating family feud. One side is eager for war; the other is resigned to it. On a battlefield, amidst the two opposing armies, moments from collision, we bear witness to an extraordinary dialogue between Krishna and Arjuna.

A paragon of virtue and integrity, Arjuna is not on the battlefield as a military conscript; by natural ability, upbringing, and conviction, he is a military leader and princely administrator. Unlike the leaders of the opposing side, he abides by the strict codes of Vedic military ethics and principles of royal governance. These statutes forbade a noble warrior from exerting his military prowess for exploitative and destructive ambitions. In current terms, that Vedic ideal would mean no suffering for the people just because their leaders are hungry for oil reserves, strategic metals, and nationalistic glory.

In India's ancient Vedic culture, ordinary civilians were neither drafted into nor directly affected by military conflicts. A professional military class waged battles in isolated areas, far from the general populace. The same persons who declared the wars had to personally fight them – on the front lines, not from the safety of remote headquarters or plush governmental chambers.

Arjuna's martial and administrative talents are dedicated exclusively to integrity, justice, and protecting the innocent. Now he has to use those skills in a most undesirable predicament. He has to fight lifelong acquaintances, kinsmen in an extended family system, and even his former teachers.

The leader of the other side – greedy, unprincipled, and morally corrupt – has refused all attempts at peaceful mediation and negotiation. Therefore, Arjuna, based on Vedic ethics, is duty bound to fight. From all angles of impartial analysis, he is clearly in the right. Nevertheless, as he surveys the enemy forces, the full impact of the dilemma suddenly hits him: he personally knows so many of the opposing warriors now resolute to kill him and his forces. Certainly, this is a crisis he would prefer to waste.

Arjuna breaks down. Soft-heartedness and compassion overtake him, and he appeals to Krishna. Backtracking from his virtuous and impeccable commitment to counter ruthless aggression, he recasts the situation: "Krishna, this battle concerns mundane politics, economics, and sociology – why do we have to go on with it? Let the other side do whatever they will. I just want to walk off the battlefield and forget it all. How agonizing, to see among the armies my family members, friends, teachers, all eager to kill one other – I can't take it. I know the other side is wrong, but if they want to be greedy, power hungry, rapacious, so be it. I just want to drop my duties, walk off the battlefield, and retire in peace."

It is as if the president of the United States or the prime minister of Australia were to announce, "Look, people, I'm tired of all the partisan politics, the ongoing legislative gridlock. I'm sick of the media and its spins. I'm out of here. Leave me alone – I'm going to be a yoga teacher."

The excuses that Arjuna gives Krishna are actually quite brilliant from economical, sociological, and political points of view. He rationalizes, "Even if my side wins, the civil havoc caused by the fatalities will be unbearable. So many men are not going home from this battlefield; their families will be shredded. Who will raise their children? Who will care for their wives? I can't be responsible for this devastating breakdown of society, just because the other side is wrong. Let them be mercenary; let their greed run its course."

87

In effect, Arjuna is saying to Krishna, "Let's forget economics, politics, sociology – let's be religious. Being pious and reverent means I walk off the battlefield with no claims to anything. I exempt myself – I don't see how any good can come out of this battle. Whether in victory or defeat, none will be happy. I know that the other side has attempted hideous assassinations and that I should stand up for justice. But they're my kin, my former friends, my old teachers – I can't do it. Though we possess every legitimate reason to fight, let's just be religious. I'll withdraw from the battlefield, retire, and live a life of noninvolvement and seclusion."

From the Vedic histories, we can understand that the character of this extraordinary personality, Arjuna, far exceeded the caliber of human beings today. So his breakdown is all the more dramatic and illustrative.

The *Gita* describes that the grief-stricken Arjuna feels his skin burning. Tears flooding his eyes, he drops his weapons and sits, depression enveloping his mind. He has all the classic symptoms of what psychologists would now call a nervous breakdown. This is crisis mode, primetime.

He implores Krishna, "We'll be pious, religious – not geopolitical."

∾ *More than Religion?* ∾

Brushing aside Arjuna's offer to be conventionally religious instead of political, Krishna responds, "Arjuna, I don't care about being religious. Let's be scientific. You think you have surpassed mundane social and political formulas by appealing to religion. But your mighty stream of erudite excuses has missed the point."

Hold on, you might say. Isn't the *Gita* a quintessential religious book, one of the world's sacred classics? Yet we hear Krishna chiding Arjuna for his lack of scientific understanding.

At this point of crisis and desperation, the *Gita* shifts into high gear. Arjuna changes his mode of interaction and enrolls in Krishna's unique academy – a transformational tutelage open to all, then and now. "I'm lost," he says, "empty of all confidence and composure. I admit I suffer from internal and external weakness. Overwhelmed by my breakdown, I'm asking you, please accept me as your subordinate, your student. Diagnose what is best for me – instruct me."

Krishna has refused to dwell on the usual religious platform of doctrines and creeds. As the Supreme Transcendence, He wants Arjuna to transcend. Therefore He initiates the discussion on the level of what actually is the real self. In this way, we can see what we should really be doing in life. Without the clear understanding of whether the self is material or nonmaterial, we can't formulate a proper response to the various crossroads of our lives.

Not wasting the crisis, but totally taking advantage of it – that is what the *Bhagavad-gita* is all about. Krishna teaches Arjuna clear-cut lessons in how the self is nonmaterial, while explicitly refuting the physico-reductionism, the matter-ism, in vogue today. Interestingly, while discarding fanatic materialistic conceptions of the self, Krishna also rejects the nihilistic and monistic notions of spiritual impersonalism and voidism.

The *Gita* is nonsectarian; readers may approach it wearing whatever label they like – this religious persuasion or that one, or none; this gender, that ethnicity, or none. You can stamp yourself as an agnostic, atheist, or true believer – even as apathetic, a popular category today that sociologists call *apa-theistic*. Regardless of your creed or affiliation, Krishna is helping you by alerting you to genuine universalism: What about us doesn't change, even as our body

and mind are always changing? This is Krishna's foundational, all-inclusive platform: "The embodied soul traverses
through the physical changes known as childhood, youth,
and old age. At death that same nonmaterial entity continues its transit, in another body. This phenomenon of nature
never bewilders the wise" (*Bhagavad-gita* 2.13).

Assuming one lives a full lifespan, who does not experience these phases of the body? What is the exact nature of
the conscious experiencer journeying through various mental and physical states? True nonsectarianism begins here.

∾ The Dogma Trail ∾

In his 2005 Stanford University commencement address,
Steve Jobs told the assembled graduating students, "Don't
be trapped by dogma – which is living with the results of
other people's thinking. Don't let the noise of others' opin-
ions drown out your own inner voice. And most important,
have the courage to follow your heart and intuition."

The prime dogma trap today is set by those who dismiss
the self as just a fantasy produced by neural activity in the
brain. There is no proof for this blind faith. Even hardcore
physicalists and contemporary philosophers admit that it's
counterintuitive for human beings to think that there is no
self, that self-identity is an illusion, and that you are just a
temporary bundle of randomness in a meaningless universe.
Though personally uncomfortable with the existence of a
nonmaterial identity, they must reluctantly acknowledge
that such a stance seems natural, even common sense.

The renowned theoretical physicist Stephen Hawking
declares the joy of utter reductionism: "The human race
is just a chemical scum on a moderate-sized planet." In my
travels on every habitable continent, I ask audiences how

many intuitively feel comfortable with that bleak materialistic proclamation of their identity. Very few ever raise their hand.

Dogma and counterintuitiveness resound in claims by Nobel-laureate biochemist Jacques Monod, known for co-discovering messenger RNA. "The ancient covenant is in pieces," he says. "Man at last knows he is alone in the unfeeling immensity of the universe, out of which he has emerged only by chance. Neither his destiny nor his duty has been written down."

Nobel laureate Francis Crick, co-discoverer of the structure of DNA, endorsed the same credo: "You, your joys and sorrows, your memories and ambitions, your sense of personal identity and free will, are, in fact, no more than the behavior of a vast assembly of nerve cells. As Lewis Carroll's Alice might have phrased it: 'You're nothing but a pack of neurons.'"

Cultural anthropologists, however, have long documented that acceptance of a self different from the body has always been ubiquitous in human society. Throughout the course of human history, most people, almost everywhere, either implicitly assume it or explicitly espouse it.

When I recently brought up Krishna's methodology for approaching science and nonsectarianism, a few people expressed their reservations: "The *Gita's* precept that all living entities are, at core, a nonmaterial particle of consciousness, unchanging though the psycho-physical packaging always changes – isn't that now deemed old-fashioned dualism, or obsolete vitalism?"

Appealing for their dispassionate deliberation, I explained that if you look through the lens of a certain restricted mindset, you can certainly view the proposition that a material body coexists with a nonmaterial self as incredulous. And it is true that our acceptance of that premise

91

would push us farther out on an apparently scary limb. We would have to face up to a universe that buzzes with both physical and nonphysical energies. To committed materialists, that acquiescence would be not only outlandishly spooky but also totally revolting.

All right – let's grant that it might be creepy to entertain the idea that a material reality coexists with a nonmaterial reality. But can we at least be impartial, if not open-minded? How spooky and miraculous is it to posit that from inanimate matter arises the strange stuff known as conscious awareness? Have you ever seen it? Can you demonstrate it in a laboratory?

Operating from the confines of a typically restricted perspective, we would have to say if this one is spooky, the other one is spooky, too. Maybe what Krishna says in the *Gita* is not so far out at all.

The materialistic theory that conscious awareness arises from chemical scum is a fantastical claim, dogmatically religious. If you can be open to that, then why not also consider Krishna's contrary contention, founded upon common sense? What is it about you that doesn't change, although your body and mind always change? Pursuing this practical angle, you get a strong indication that there is at least *something* outside the box, something nonmaterial about you.

Despite the intuitiveness of the common-sense approach, you may retort that an indication, no matter how much it is validated by common sense, doesn't equate to scientific fact; just because Krishna says something doesn't make it true.

Now we reach a crucial juncture: Krishna's identity – the axis upon which the *Bhagavad-gita* revolves. An open-minded reader of the *Gita*, reaching this station, will choose to remain on the train and receive an education in exactly who Krishna is.

What's more, throughout the *Gita*, Krishna supplies us with spiritual laboratory techniques for verifying the existence of nonmaterial reality. Nowhere in the *Gita* does He say, "I want you to believe this; all you have to do is believe." Rather, throughout, He volunteers, "Here is the procedure for verifying what I'm saying; Now listen as I explain how by practicing *bhakti*, yoga in full consciousness, you can know fully who I am, free from doubt" (7.1).

The most competent instructor, Krishna checks up on Arjuna at the end of the *Gita*: "Have you heard this most authoritative yoga science with an attentive mind? Are your ignorance and illusion now dispelled?" (18.72).

Arjuna's final feedback to his eternal friend who has become his guru: "Dearest Krishna, O infallible, my illusion is now finished. Your applied spiritual technology has returned my original consciousness. Unshakable and free from doubt, I am ready to execute. Your plan is my plan" (18.73).

The crisis is not wasted.

❧ Enough of the Spiritual – Other Options? ❧

The *Gita* demonstrates the trajectory of a crisis that commences on the ground, the geopolitical and socioeconomic level, then falters on the routine religious level, and finally reaches its resolution on the transcendental, nonmaterial level. Despite Arjuna's breakdown at the onset, he accepts Krishna's methodology and triumphs.

Turning a blind eye to Krishna's nonmaterial solutions, we can gallantly pursue the usual material options. Many scholars and scientists have concluded that the global crises now upon us demonstrate that human psychological capability has not kept pace with human technological might.

While our technology has advanced to impressive heights, our nature has remained mired. The result: we are not in control of our technology or ourselves. From all perspectives – social, political, economical – we're not only stuck but also doing ourselves in, expertly.

One obvious symptom of our internal malignancy is humanity's inability to reverse its ruinous impact on the environment. But the advancement in horribly destructive weapons is also out of control.

Back in the twentieth century, fears of weapons of mass destruction centered upon the traditional terrible nuclear, biological and chemical (NBC) armaments. Entry into the nuclear club had a hefty price: rare raw materials and forbidden information. Effective biological and chemical weapons generally required both sizable industrial complexes and operational expertise.

Reflecting "progress" in the twenty-first century, the *Bulletin* of the Atomic Scientists reports 16,300 nuclear weapons located at ninety-eight sites in fourteen countries – enough to kill all of humanity many times over. Most of the weaponry resides in the United States and Russia. But twenty-five countries warehouse enough materials to build a nuclear weapon, and many of these storehouses are vulnerable to plunder.

And more destructive wonders await us. Current work in genetics, nanotechnology, and robotics (GNR) heralds an entirely new set of frights. While big nations struggle to bottle up the NBC weapons, the new GNR advancements open the way for accidents and demonic abuse by individuals and small groups. Concerned scientists warn that GNR requires no large production facilities or exotic raw materials – just knowledge.

Bill Joy, cofounder and chief scientist of Sun Microsystems, was co-chair of the presidential commission on the future of IT research. In *Wired* magazine at the turn of the century, looking into the coming decades, he warned about GNR: "I think it is no exaggeration to say we are on the cusp of the further perfection of extreme evil, an evil whose possibility spreads well beyond that which weapons of mass destruction bequeathed to the nation-states, on to a surprising and terrible empowerment of extreme individuals."

More recently, Stephen Hawking has confirmed such fears, pointing particularly to advances in robotics as a threat to our very existence. "The development of full artificial intelligence could spell the end of the human race," he told the BBC in December 2014. "Humans, who are limited by slow biological evolution, couldn't compete and would be superseded."

What happened to the development of human character? As noted earlier, the panorama of environmental, social, and economic problems testify to an institutional problem, but the institutional challenges attest to humans who are challenged. For example, ecological economists, that new breed, say the time has long come for us to accept that global economic issues are not really about economics, as narrowly conceived. They are a moral problem; business as usual won't suffice.

The key question is how human beings can have economic growth in a way that doesn't imperil planet Earth, our habitat and life-support system.

When speaking recently at the London School of Business, I brought up the best-selling treatise *The Price of Civilization* by Jeffrey Sachs, a globetrotting megastar macroeconomist who has usually focused on poverty in the developing world. Now he has reset his sights on the United States, where he is director of Columbia University's Earth Institute.

Sachs's book and subsequent talks brilliantly analyze

the socio-economic gamut of America's predicament: the dramatic disparities in wealth, the politics driven by big money, and the citizens sunk into their TV screens while being fleeced by the clever and powerful. "America," he writes, "has developed the world's most competitive market society but has squandered its civic virtue along the way. Without restoring an ethos of social responsibility, there can be no meaningful and sustained economic recovery."

Sachs's final verdict: the American public and its leaders need to understand once again the values of moderation, cooperation, collaboration, compassion, and virtue. The United States has a crisis in personal character.

Hearing this diagnosis of national disease aroused eagerness for a remedy. The business magazine *Fortune* commented, "While no reasonable person would disagree, it's less clear how this great renewal is supposed to come about."

Reporters at a news conference in New York asked for a treatment plan. Cutting across all lines of class, ethnicity, and ideology, how can the nation retool its traits? What is the healing process for regenerating such a basic, universal fiber of ethics? Sachs replied, "That's not my department – I'm an economist."

❧ *Global Collective Quagmire* ❧

Will a sudden spurt in our evolution save humanity from itself? Don't hold your breath. Behavioral evolutionists say that while nature's pace of selection is plodding, our pace of technological proliferation is increasing at breakneck speed. As a result, we are magnificently adapted to a world that no longer exists.

They say that physically, psychologically, socially, and

through our moral dispositions, we match up well with the
prehistoric characteristics of nomadic hunter-gatherers on
the African savannah. Back then, humans are thought to
have needed social skills for interaction within tribal en-
claves of only fifty to one hundred persons. Living close
to the earth and tilling the land in small groups, humans
worked out their social issues within their immediate
circles.

We can all agree that we no longer live in such a world.
Instead of primitive tools scratching a few acres, applied
science now alters the entire planet, detonating geophysical repercussions far into the future.

Rather than looking for as-yet-unwritten treatises, we
can turn again to the ancient *Bhagavad-gita*, which actually anticipates current humanity's syndrome of self-
annihilation posing as prosperity and progress. In the *Gita*
Krishna explains:

> The depraved, with their twisted mentalities, pre-
> sume the world is a phantasmagoric accident, arising
> from random interactions of matter – no ultimate
> foundation, no support, no ultimate controller. They
> think only selfish instincts and desires perpetuate it.
>
> Based on this doctrine, such lost creatures, vi-
> sion darkened, specializing in nescience, perpetrate
> not only malicious deeds but also horrendous works,
> capable of havoc on the scale of world destruction.
> (16.8–9)

Our predicament is that climate change, combined with
cutting-edge weaponry of global obliteration, threatens
not just a few prehistoric nomadic encampments scattered
here and there, but all of the earth and its inhabitants.

Since the agricultural revolution, conventionally dated eight thousand years ago, the human population is said to have increased a thousandfold.

Have we former tribals, our numbers multiplied exponentially, long lost the capability to resolve our social problems? No doubt, the acceleration of scientific change, especially in the past two centuries, has been extraordinary. But what about our capacity for moral psychology – does it match our dazzling technological might?

We have major problems, we are told, because our moral dispositions are the same as back when humans were to have emerged as *Homo sapiens*.

First, the human moral compass and ethical capacity have not evolved to the point where we can effectively consider the welfare of strangers, outsiders – anyone beyond our immediate kinship group or hunter-gatherer circle. In social interactions, our present stage of moral development renders feeble our attempts to feel significant empathy or guilt for humans not near and similar to us. To our moral conscience, the "out-group" members are mere shadows. What's more, their sufferings are minimized and their mistakes are magnified. Hence, the nightmare of nationalistic wars and genocide continue.

Our second inability is that we haven't attained the ability to consider impacts affecting the far future – we deal adroitly with only immediate crises. "Environmental calamities kicking in at the end of the century? What – me worry? The risk is eons away. Besides, the humans who assume control of the earth a century from now are unknown entities to us – phantoms of futurism."

A third deficiency is that if we feel we are not individually or directly the cause of the problem, we assign ourselves markedly less personal blame. When the outcomes of our individual actions merge with those of the masses, we aren't singled out, and we duck culpability for what is done by the throng. Neither you nor I personally set off global warming. We don't work in a laboratory for researching WMDS or GNRS. So why take it all so personally?

Arousing even less individual remorse than acts of large-scale commission are acts of societal omission: "We didn't instigate this social injustice. True, we watched it proliferate and did nothing to prevent it; but we didn't cause it."

Human crises have escalated well beyond local village dilemmas. Our momentous modern plights, connecting all regions, are now crowned "global collective action problems." Wherefrom does global humanity find the will and tenacity to enable the required momentous international cooperation? Global collective action necessitates qualities of trusting and helping faceless strangers far from our home. But apparently we are wired to be suspicious, even xenophobic, toward people outside our tribal enclave or neighborhood.

❧ Better Living through Biochemicals ❧

Can technology, though pushing us to the brink of military and ecological disaster, offer a saving grace? Some leading scholars and scientists are touting, as our last hope, mass-scale application of "biomedical moral enhancement."

Since human beings are just a walking cask of chemicals and are especially chemically driven in the brain, they say, why not administer appropriate neurochemicals that modify human behavior, boosting the population en masse? Through biomedical tinkering, we could fast-forward beyond sluggish evolutionary development. Enhanced humans would immediately be more altruistic, sacrificial, and empathetic, and world peace and ecological sanity might have a chance.

The idea is that if we are to avoid impending human disaster, we've got to explore every potential solution at hand – even by pressing into service what is still experimental and novel. Our crisis is so monumental that if we roll the dice on biomedical moral enhancement, we've everything to gain and nothing to lose.

Who could possibly propose such a massive artificial intervention? Crackpot, fringe scientists? No, or at least not unless you include in that category Professor Julian Savulescu, Director of the Oxford Uehiro Centre for Practical Ethics and Oxford's Institute of Science and Ethics, and editor of the *Journal of Medical Ethics*, ranked by Google Scholar Metrics as the leading journal in the field. Or Ingmar Persson, Professor of Practical Philosophy at the University of Gothenburg, also a participant in Oxford's Uehiro Centre.

Outside the lecture halls and inside the actual laboratories, biomedical engineers admit that the technology of moral enhancement is still in its infancy. What's more, they issue no guarantee that the appropriate research will mature in time to save humanity from itself. They simply assert that because the required moral modification is now theoretically feasible, our inherited biology and genetics do not immutably doom us to wiping ourselves out.

The Oxford academics present their case: "Our knowledge of human biology – in particular of genetics and neurobiology – is beginning to enable us to directly affect the biological or physiological bases of human motivation, either through drugs, or through genetic selection or engineering, or by using external devices that affect the brain or the learning process. We could use these techniques to overcome the moral and psychological shortcomings that imperil the human species. We are at the early stages of such research, but there are few cogent philosophical or moral objections to the use of specifically *biomedical* moral enhancement – or *moral bioenhancement*. ... We simply can't afford to miss opportunities."

Humans already resort to pharmacological enhancers for diverse aspects of life. Athletes use them to increase their competitive edge; academics, their cognitive powers; people in general, their lusty indulgences. Pedophiles are given anti-libidinal drugs to reduce their sex drive. And don't forget the millions throughout the world relying upon antidepressants to ameliorate their behavior by adjusting neurochemical imbalances in the brain.

So why squirm when contemplating employing biochemicals to upgrade moral qualities? By the grace of oxytocin and selective serotonin reuptake inhibitors, proponents tell us, you could push up your altruistic dispositions and sense of justice. The latest generation of antidepressants has been discovered to award a corollary bonus: they also decrease aggressive, impulsive behavior and increase placidity in social dealings. The resultant easy-goingness is said to enable more cooperativeness, leading to social synergism, collaboration, and compromise. Wouldn't humanity benefit from such a heightened inner predilection for harmony, a crucial and desperately needed moral quality, in a world under the gun of crises demanding global collective action?

Chemical-enhancement advocates remind us that we cannot be rescued by politics alone. Political affairs derive from the human personality and accordingly reflect the limitations of the human character. Since humanity's inner development has lagged dangerously behind its external technological prowess, politics will not be the solution.

Economic redemption? Everyone knows that Wall

Street is not for sadhus and sages. Free-market democracy has turned out to mean, "Can you swim with the sharks?" As for socialism, "It works fine if everyone is a saint, but if all are saints, who needs socialism?"

What about good old moral education? "God says this is good, this is bad." Won't that save the day? The bioenhancement camp asserts that although religious morality has been around for thousands of years, scant evidence exists of significant, large-scale, enduring behavioral modification. Despite many undeniably great moral teachers throughout the ages, humanity still lacks even the basic ethical skills to ensure its survival, or that of the earth.

A practical look at history, both religious and secular, reveals a species that doesn't seem capable of walking its moral talk. At best, we solemnly recite moral platitudes in public and then abandon them in private.

Recognizing the in-built limitations of human psychology, should we then embrace all the scientific possibilities at our command? Employing appropriate knowledge of the brain and its chemistry, we could assist, rather than replace, traditional moral education. This would improve not only our moral performance, but our politics, economics, and any system based on human character – in short, anything human.

In 2011, Professor Savulescu concluded on Australian national radio:

> What I believe we should also do is look at enhancing our moral dispositions ... by understanding the biological revolution that I described. I'm not arguing that we shouldn't employ education, psychology, political strategy, social interventions, etc. We should do all of those things – the problem is so great. But it's time to look not just outside to what we can do

outside but to inside and how we can look to improve ourselves not just by reading Socrates or Buddha or the Bible but also by looking at how we're disposed to relate to other people and to react in the world.

In other words, let the biochemicals inwardly alter human disposition; then our relations and reactions in the outer world may finally change. Give neurochemical upliftment a full go.

The biomedical solution, however, is not without its drawbacks. *Srimad-Bhagavatam* issues us a clear warning:

> O greatest, O Supreme, our actual status in the material world means constantly meeting with appealing and unappealing situations and separation from them. Whether supposedly heavenly or hellish, any predicament in a material body in the material world is actually most deplorable; therefore we burn in a fire of lamentation. Although we expertly fabricate countless remedies to counter the miseries of life, these so-called solutions in the material world eventually reveal themselves as more problematic than the predicaments they're designed to resolve. Therefore the only real cure-all is to engage in *bhakti-yoga*. (7.9.17)

The first problem with biomedical moral enhancement, as even its propagators admit, is that the very persons advancing this technology as a solution are likely the ones most in need of the biochemicals to straighten themselves out. The panacea of moral enhancement has to be administered by morally imperfect creatures, dogged by the same problems they are seeking to cure in others. Bioenhancer, heal thyself.

We can appreciate the bioethicists for fingering the

crux of the human plight. But either desperation or good fortune may push us to consider higher-level solutions. Excelling in our wholesale crisis of temporary existence in a temporary world, the *Bhagavad-gita* supplies the know-how for producing a wisdom culture, an individual and mass mindset based on the self-controlled mind and senses and a flawless vision of nature, its assets, and its proprietor.

The *Gita* advocates a spiritually flourishing lifestyle based on our comprehending the nonmaterial nature of the self fully in relation to the Supreme Self. Remember Krishna's core definition of illusion: consciously or implicitly construing ourselves as matter, we strategize to appease and satisfy the body and mind through material positioning and alignment.

How can we free ourselves of that illusion? Krishna's concluding instruction, the most important in the *Gita*, is that rather than relying on our limited intelligence to resolve these deeply seated and far-reaching issues, we turn for plans and designs to the ultimate, supreme source of all energy. Transcendental knowledge recognizes the existence of limited consciousness as well as unlimited consciousness, and it advocates that we revive the eternal relationship between the two.

✀ *Superconscious Connection* ✀

Krishna's interactive session leaves us with clear instructions: "Arjuna, you are limited consciousness; I am unlimited consciousness. We're meant to function together like the part functions with the whole. You are the finite; I am the infinite. If you forget about Me, you're in illusion. Imagining your separateness from Me, thinking you're the body and the mind, dreaming that the world and its resources are yours, you'll never achieve natural happiness, peace, or progress. Listen to Me, follow My techniques, and you will come out of illusion. Only then can you actually see how to benefit yourself and all living beings."

The *bhakti-yoga* process presented in the *Gita* can serve as a nonmaterial methodology for extricating us from delusion and returning us to original pure levels of consciousness, distinct from material misidentification in our conceptions and goals. This is the timeless luxury that fulfills our natural, genuine desires.

"Shape your life so you are always conscious of Me. Offer all your love, endeavors, and reverence to Me. Surely, in pure yoga you will reunite with Me. I promise you this because you're My own intimate part, My beloved, My very dear friend." (*Bhagavad-gita* 18.64)

About the Author

Devamrita Swami is an American-born educator, author and sannyasi, monk, in the Krishna *bhakti* tradition. For over 40 years, he has been travelling the world sharing the teachings and lifestyle of *bhakti-yoga*.

Upon graduating from Yale University, he began reading and relishing the classic bhakti texts translated by His Divine Grace A. C. Bhaktivedanta Swami Prabhupada, the Founder-Acharya of the International Society for Krishna Consciousness (ISKCON). Impressed by his impeccable erudition and saintliness, Devamrita Swami became his official student and a member of the worldwide *bhakti* community.

Often addressing topics on spiritually based economics, sustainability, and environmentalism, his strategic guidance has proved invaluable to students and professionals seeking to balance their spiritual and professional life. With a unique ability to analyze modern problems through the wisdom of the *Bhagavad-gita* and *Srimad-Bhagavatam* (essential Vedic texts), he challenges audiences to understand that the quest for genuine personal and social upliftment is rooted in precise and comprehensive knowledge. Spiritual life, he often remarks, is a dynamic experiential reality, not a token subscription to a belief-system.

Adept at applying this spiritual science, he encourages others to enter the laboratory and perform the Krishna experiment, which enables us to fully realize our nonmaterial identity and ultimate connection.

While meeting and relishing the diversity of global humanity, he has also established urban and rural sanctuaries for the spiritually inquisitive, especially in New Zealand.

Other books he has authored include *Searching for Vedic India* and *Perfect Escape.*

www.devamritaswami.com